£2

C000099358

BRISTOL'S LOST CITY

Built to inspire
Transformed for war

Clive Burlton

BRISTOL BOOKS

Bristol Books CIC, 1 Lyons Court, Long Ashton Business Park,
Yanley Lane, Long Ashton, Bristol BS41 9LB

Bristol's Lost City: Built to Inspire Transformed for War by Clive Burlton

Published by Bristol Books 2014

ISBN 978-1-909446-05-02

Copyright: Bristol Books CiC

Design: Joe Burt (joe@wildsparkdesign.com)

Clive Burlton has asserted his right under the Copyright, Designs and Patents Act of
1988 to be identified as the author of this work.

All rights reserved. This book may not be reproduced or transmitted in any form
or in any means without the prior written consent of the publisher, except by a
reviewer who wishes to quote brief passages in connection with a review written in
a newspaper or magazine or broadcast on television, radio or on the internet.

A CIP record for this book is available from the British Library

ABOUT THE AUTHOR

Clive Burlton, a born-and-bred Bristolian, is an author, publisher and social historian. In 2011 he wrote Trenches to Trams (Tangent Books), the story of George Pine, a Bristol Tommy who served with the Gloucesters during the First World War.

A volunteer at Bristol Record Office since 2008, Clive co-founded Bristol Books in 2012 and he's a non-executive director of Empica Ltd.

His other books include Wading through the Years (Bristol Books) which marked the 40th anniversary of Wessex Water and Bravo, Bristol! – The City at War 1914-1918 (Redcliffe Press) co-writtten with Eugene Byrne.

ACKNOWLEDGEMENTS

With grateful thanks to the staff at Bristol Record Office and the Bristol Library Service for their help and advice and allowing access to documents, maps, sketches, manuscripts and photographs. Bristol should really do more to appreciate and recognise the specialisms that are at risk with the cost cutting measures taking place across these essential historical research services.

A big thank you to Eugene Byrne, Peter John, Dean Marks and Andy Stevens of Pastimes for making me aware of various aspects of the White City site and to Richard Burley for his early encouragement to do this book. Thanks also to Andrew and Melanie Kelly and the rest of the Bristol 2014 project for their valuable help and support.

Thank you to the Bristol Post for the appeals in Bristol Times which yielded some lovely additional stories and images.

A final thank you to the following for their help, advice and support and where noted in the Picture Credits on page 96 for allowing me to reproduce images under their custodianship or ownership: Jane Bradley, Alison Brown, Joe Burt, Matt Coles, Allie Dillon, Dawn Dyer, David Emeney, Sue Giles, Simon Harding, Ruth Hecht, Pete Insole, Richard Jones, Catherine Littlejohns, Karen MacDonald, John Penny, Martin Powell, David Read and the Soldiers of Gloucestershire Museum, Pamela Steed, Andy Stevens, Sue Stops, Graham Tratt, Julian Warren and the National Archives at Kew.

INTRODUCTION

The motivation for telling one of Bristol's great untold stories goes back several years. Busily researching my wife's grandfather's memoirs for Trenches to Trams (Tangent Books, 2011), I was shown a photograph of my grandfather with dozens of other young Bristol soldiers in front of what looked like a castle.

Stanley Barnes was one of the volunteer recruits who helped to form 'Bristol's Own' at the start of the First World War in 1914. Perhaps the location was where they were in training at Wensleydale in Yorkshire, or Saltburn near Sunderland, or Codford on Salisbury Plain, or even a chateaux in France or outside an extravagant billet in Belgium?

No, this was Bristol in 1914. I knew Oliver Cromwell had flattened the original castle in the 1600s. Why did I not know about the 1914 variety? Fact is, very few local folk are familiar with the replica structures and strikingly white pavilions that sprang up in a frenzied ten-week period of construction between March and 28th May 1914 when the Bristol International Exhibition opened.

Close up, and from vantage points like Bedminster Down and Clifton Suspension Bridge the views were extraordinary – no wonder the site was coined, 'White City'.

Designed to be inspirational, the exhibition was a financial disaster. The key civic and commercial leaders in Bristol didn't engage with the project soon enough or in most cases, not at all. At the time, Bristol was more concerned with strengthening trading links with Britain's Dominions and attracting business to the Port of Bristol, than supporting an international exhibition carrying its name.

Stung by being criticised for 'petty jealousies' and 'small minded provincialism', Bristol finally got behind the exhibition, but it was too late. A winding-up petition was already in front of the Bristol County Court when the storm clouds over Europe burst with the declaration of war on 4th August 1914.

The world was about to change forever. The transformation was poignantly played out at the White City site where the exhibition to showcase Britain's Empire was closed for good and the War Office turned the site into a barracks for Bristol's volunteer recruits.

The story of Bristol's White City, is lost no longer.

Clive Burlton

CONTENTS

PART 1

WHITE CITY EXHIBITION

PRE-WAR 1914

Bristol International Exhibition Limited was incorporated as a company with a nominal share capital of 2,000 shares valued at £1 each on 24th May 1912 – two years before the exhibition opened. Although most of the ideas and most of the money to fund the exhibition came from outside Bristol, it was three local entrepreneurs who completed the legalities to establish the company in the first place: Edward Lovell was an engineer from Chesterfield Road in Montpelier; Eliza Love was a building contractor from Hampton Road, Redland and Frederick Jones was another engineer living on the Wells Road in Knowle.

Lovell and Jones were joined as initial directors of the company by accountant Charles Howes of 30 Bushy Park, Knowle and George Parfitt, who was a consulting electrical engineer of Priory Road in Keynsham. Howes had in fact been working on the project in an unpaid capacity since 25th March 1912 and it was his idea to stage a Pageant of Bristol to run alongside a 'colonial exhibition'.

Within a year of formation, and a year before the exhibition was due to open, all founding directors of the exhibition company had resigned. They stayed as directors long enough to appoint a successor management team. Most of the former directors signed separate agreements and were awarded contracts for work on the exhibition. Part of their remuneration included the allotment of shares in the Exhibition Company and participation in a scheme to pay commission based on exhibition profits/receipts once the exhibition had ended.

The management of the exhibition became the responsibility of two newly appointed directors who were not West Country men - John Bellham and Leolyn

Leolyn Gustav Hart, preparing for the Exhibition.

Gustav Hart were both from London.

Bellham described himself as a Colonial Merchant and was appointed Space and Concessions Director to handle the sales and marketing side of the venture and Leolyn Hart, a Theatrical Manager, was appointed General Manager and Technical Director.

Leolyn Hart was well-known in theatrical circles, being a renowned, respected and sought-after scenic artist and director. He set up his own scenery painting company in the 1880s and worked across the country – in theatres, on pageants, on pantomimes, on piers and in music halls. Provincial newspapers and the 'Era' magazine - for theatre goers – reported regularly on his grand schemes, spectacular stage sets and visual scenes from the late 1880s through to the late 1920s. With a career spanning some 50 years, he knew his stuff.

Hart's work on the massive Festival of Empire at Crystal Palace in London in 1911 came to the attention of the Bristol entrepreneurs who set up the Bristol International Exhibition Company in 1912. In fact it was they who approached Hart after the Festival of Empire and invited him to take on the Directorship of the Bristol Exhibition.

Hart's work in London in 1911 had quite a bearing on the plans he drew up to stage the most ambitious and spectacular exhibition the West Country had ever seen. Other attractions in Bristol would include 'Shakespeare's England' – a major draw when it was exhibited at Earls Court in 1912.

The early public statements from Hart and Bellham about the Bristol International Exhibition were quite clear about its purpose: *'Not only is it to be a place of pleasure and delight, but it aims at being a great object lesson of Empire and its meaning, bringing to the eye the resourcefulness and progress of Great Britain and her Dominions in a manner such as only an Exhibition of its scope and magnitude can accomplish.'*

Although local engineering, building and electrical contractors could see the opportunities for participation in a major construction project, with promises of business and potential riches, Bristol's civic elite appeared more guarded.

Despite 'cordial' support for the international exhibition, which was not its idea, Bristol was already doing very nicely, thank you, with its relationships with Britain's Overseas Dominions. Did it really want others to muscle-in on its territory and did it really want an exhibition modelled on those in the metropolis, to be plonked on its doorstep? Initially, the jury was out and in any case, Bristol had other things on its mind…

THE ROYAL AGRICULTURAL SHOW – JULY 1913

As Leolyn Hart and John Bellham set about the task of staging the exhibition - putting the funding in place, negotiating contracts with suppliers and trying to find a suitable site to hold it - Bristol was already immersed in helping to organise another huge high-profile event.

In 1910, Bristol offered to host the Royal Agricultural Society's annual exhibition and got its wish in 1913 by hosting the 74th Royal Agricultural Show which was held on Durdham Downs from 1st to 5th July - the third time the annual agricultural show had come to the city. Around 70,000 visitors attended each day.

Many prominent citizens were involved in organising the event, including Sir Frank Wills JP, a respected local architect. Sir Frank was a member of the WD & HO Wills tobacco family dynasty, a City Councillor and in 1911-12 was Lord Mayor of Bristol. Sir Frank chaired the Local Executive Committee of the Agricultural Show. He had a keen interest in agriculture and was active in forging relations with Britain's Dominions. Whilst Lord Mayor in 1912 he visited Nova Scotia with a group of civic leaders and industrialists including Palliser Martin and Henry L Riseley JP.

Palliser Martin was a hemp and flax merchant, a politician and member of the Bristol Chamber of that Bristol had with Canada.

Developing relations with the Dominions for the benefit of Bristol's commercial interests was something Henry Riseley and Palliser Martin were particular good and experienced at. In 1909 for example, Riseley and Martin, toured Australia and New Zealand extolling the benefits of trade with Bristol and the use of the improved facility at Avonmouth and its new Royal Edward Dock that opened in 1908. Since that trade mission, most shipping agents and ministers from Australia and New Zealand had visited Bristol to see for themselves the facilities on offer.

Against this background, Henry Riseley took it upon himself to organise a specific Overseas Dominions section for the 1913 Royal Agricultural Show. Already a member of Sir Frank's Local Executive Committee, he set up an Overseas Dominions Committee to co-ordinate the arrangements and source the exhibits for this section of the Show. Through his efforts, the following were represented at the Show: the Department of Agriculture, Bengal, India; the Canadian Government Emigration Department; the Canadian Northern Railway; the Canadian Pacific Railway; the Commonwealth of Australia; the Victoria Government; the Western Australia Government; the South Australian Government; the Queensland Government; the Orient Line of Steamers; the Union of South Africa; the British South Africa Company; the Government of the Federated Malay States; the West India Committee with exhibits from Jamaica, Grenada, St Lucia, British Guiana and British Honduras; the

Palliser Martin, Lady and Sir Frank Wills, R E Bush and Henry Riseley.

Commerce. Representing Bristol's interests, he also served on several national organisations that promoted Britain's trading links with the rest of the world. He was also Chairman of the Bristol Musical Festival. Henry Riseley, an insurance broker, was Sheriff in 1905, was President of the Society of Bristolians in London and was Chairman of the Bristol Publicity Committee. At the time, Riseley was regarded as Bristol's Chief Spokesman.

During the visit to Halifax, Nova Scotia, a tablet showing John Cabot leaving Bristol was placed in the Tower in the town that was built to commemorate the grant of legislative powers upon the provinces of Nova Scotia. The Bristol party was entertained by the Montreal Chamber of Commerce and the visit continued to cement the long-standing commercial and cultural relationships

Sir Frank Wills outside the Commonwealth of Australia stand at the Royal Agricultural Show in 1913.

Dominions Settlement Association; and the Port of Bristol Authority.

On Friday 4th July 1913, the Show was attended by King George V who made a point of referring to the new section in the show during his address:

'I learn with interest of the introduction, for the first time, of a section illustrating the processes of agriculture in my Overseas Dominions. It is gratifying to find this section originates in the City of Bristol, which has been so long and honourably connected with many of the Dominions, and I have no doubt that it will serve not a little to strengthen those bonds of mutual help and affection which so happily exist between the various parts of my Empire'.

The success of the Show and its new Overseas Dominions section probably gave Henry Riseley the idea to repeat one of the trade missions he undertook with Palliser Martin some years previously. As Riseley set about the planning for his next ambassadorial adventure, arrangements were gradually taking shape for the Bristol International Exhibition…

COUNTDOWN TO THE 1914 EXTRAVAGANZA

As Hart and Bellham put in place arrangements for suppliers to provide services, the number of shares allotted to contractors continued to grow. Local architects, engineers, builders, accountants, wallpaper merchants, chemical manufacturers, yeast merchants, printers and amusement callers, were all engaged to provide services and received an allocation of shares, either in place of cash/cheque payments or as part of their overall remuneration.

Appointments to some of the key roles included:

Charles Howes of Bushy Park, Knowle - Exhibition Organiser

George Jefferies of Nailsea - Company Secretary and Cashier

George Parfitt of Keynsham - Consulting Electrical Engineer

David Lewes of London – Consulting Engineer

Frederick Jones of Cotham Brow - Engineer

Dr Frank Merrick of Clifton - Chairman of the Musical Committee

George Riseley of Clifton - Secretary to the Musical Committee

William Fowler of Tyndalls Park - Secretary of the Musical Competitions

Ralph Lewin, Royal West of England Fine Arts Academy - Secretary to the Fine Arts Committee

William Jones of Redland – Secretary to Leolyn Hart and Press/Publicity Representative

John Henderson of London – Master of the Pageant

Blanche Beatrice Barber of Clifton – Secretary to the Pageant

Jennie Cornwallis-West of London – Designer and adviser for 'Shakespeare's England'

With the initial allotment of shares now exhausted, the company increased the nominal share capital by a further 8,000 shares valued at £1 each. George Parfitt, who had spent a lot of time on planning the electricity requirements for the eventual site, was re-appointed a Director of the company, having previously resigned.

SITE ACQUIRED

The site the organisers settled on to hold the exhibition was at a place sometimes known as 'Ashton Fields', 'Ashton Meadows' or 'Rownham Fields' - a huge swathe of land on the south side of the River Avon, near Ashton Swing Bridge and opposite 'B' Bond Warehouse.

The 30-acre site was owned partly by the City Corporation (7 acres) and partly by the Great Western Railway Company (23 acres).

The Exhibition Company signed an agreement with the City Corporation on 15th May 1913 to lease the land from 24th June 1913 until 31st December 1914. Rent was set at £150 per year, payable on signing the agreement with a second payment due on 24th June 1914. A similar agreement was reached with the Great Western Railway Company in November 1913 for the lease of its land.

PUBLICITY GETS UNDERWAY

With the site now acquired, William Jones, a journalist from Redland, Bristol, could now get the publicity machinery in motion. He immediately pressed the 'Go'

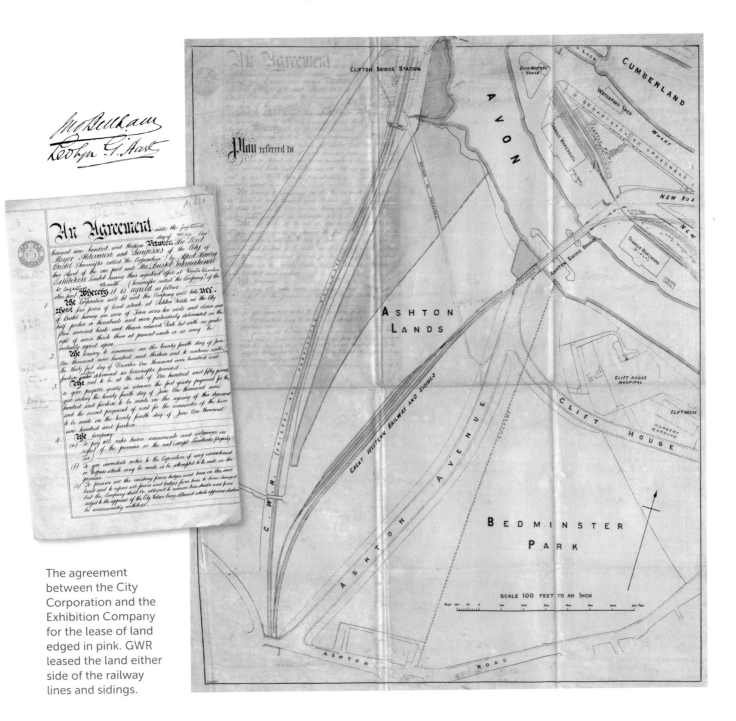

The agreement between the City Corporation and the Exhibition Company for the lease of land edged in pink. GWR leased the land either side of the railway lines and sidings.

button on publicising the event and issued press releases to news organisations across the country. The day after the agreements for leasing the site were signed, articles started to appear in newspapers and magazines. The 17th May 1913 edition of the *Cheltenham Looker-On* was typical of the coverage…

"INTERNATIONAL EXHIBITION AT BRISTOL.
ENCHANTING PLEASURE CITY ON AVON'S BANK.
EDUCATIONAL AND COMMERCIAL
UNDERTAKING.

◆

It may appear premature to talk about an Exhibition to be held in 1914, but Exhibitions which are designed upon an international character, and upon the lines of the recent elaborate Exhibitions of the Metropolis, necessitate many months of preparation.

For the Bristol International Exhibition, which will be held from May until October next year, arrangements have long been proceeding, and although twelve months still separate us from the time of opening, the Grounds at Ashton Gate, Bristol, already bear witness to activities upon a large scale.

Bristol should make a favourable centre for a great Exhibition, easily accessible as it is by train from all parts of the Midlands and the West Country, and also by steamboat from the Bristol Channel and South Wales. The buildings embraced in the Exhibition scheme will be many and novel in character. The central feature will be the International Building 250 feet high, the design being a huge globe 60 feet in diameter, set upon a cascade of real water which will tumble down a stepped-pyramidal roof which, in its turn, is supported upon a bold base of

Babylonian treatment.

Whether by day, or by night, when this magnificent building is illuminated by the kaleidoscopic rays of powerful electric lights, this International Building will prove an attractive landmark for travellers approaching Bristol. Here will be housed a comprehensive collection of international exhibits, including a Fine Art section entirely devoted to modern works of art, and also general exhibits of all nations as distinct from our Colonies.

The Overseas Dominions will be represented by exhibits from their resources and industries, displayed in two ornate buildings, and there is the prospect of all our Dominions being represented, particularly, perhaps, Canada and Australia. Other buildings will be the Machinery Pavilion, with a floor area of 60,000 feet, of novel and curious construction, being composed of thousands of various parts of machinery, its decorative pillars taking the form of bright steel shafting's and spindles, and their caps and bases will be cog and fly wheels, and so on; the Military Pavilion, a reproduction of Bristol's ancient Castle, which was demolished by command of Oliver Cromwell 270 years ago, and which will therefore have much interest for Bristol and general visitors, beyond the attractiveness of the contents of the building, a collection of military loan exhibits of intense interest because of its historical associations; the Naval and Marine Pavilion, the exterior of which will take the form of one of Britain's latest battleships, and which will be full of historical, naval and marine exhibits, from Government Departments and private collections; and the Concert Pavilion, too, unique in construction, and designed to yield the utmost comfort and pleasure, instead of stuffiness and oppression usually inseparable from such buildings in the heat of summer.

In the Concert Pavilion, musical festivals and competitions will be of frequent occurrence, and the Music Committee of the Exhibition under the chairmanship of Dr Frank Merrick, have compiled a programme of concerts and band music which cannot fail to please every visitor who has the smallest musical taste. There will be Refreshment Rooms dispersed throughout the Grounds and a Garden Club, from which an exquisite view of the beautifully trimmed lawns and luxurious flower beds will be obtained. Indeed, the gardens of the Exhibition will be an education in themselves, laid out and decorated as they will be by a firm of the highest reputation amongst horticulturalists and landscape gardeners.

Shakespeare's England will be represented in a section of the grounds by reproductions of the quaint houses of the period, the inns, taverns, a theatre, the village green upon which Morris and Maypole dances will be kept up and all the life and picturesqueness of Elizabethan days will here be maintained under the controlling hand of Mrs. George Cornwallis West, responsible for the magnificent Shakespeare's England at Earls Court.

Another interesting feature of the Exhibition will be Revenge, Drake's famous flagship, the loss of which in a glorious encounter with the Spaniards, which encompassed the death of Sir Richard Grenville, has been so splendidly told in verse by Tennyson.

And added to all the attractiveness of these comprehensive exhibits there will be the great "Pageant of Bristol and the West," to be produced by thousands of local people under the direction of Mr. John Henderson, one of the greatest Masters of Pageant in the World, and which will be witnessed by delighted crowds from a Grand

Stand capable of accommodating nearly 4,000 people. The Pageant Ground will also be utilised for a children's "Pageant of Fairy Land" in which some 2,000 Bristol children will be engaged.

When Pageantry is not being produced, the Pageant Ground will be devoted to International Sports, the programme embracing many events which will attract visitors from long distances, and which are being organised by a Sports Committee, of whom Lord Desborough is the President. The Amusements section of the Exhibition will be one of the most attractive of modern times, for there will be assembled all the up to date devices over which three continents have gone wild. The latest scientific and mechanical amusements will be available here, and there will frequently be as much fun to be enjoyed from watching other people's "thrills" as there will be in experiencing them for oneself.

The scheme of Illumination of the Exhibition Buildings and Grounds by night will be gorgeous and magnificent, so that either by day or by night, the spectacle will be one which visitors will long remember.

The boldness of the scheme upon which the Exhibition is being formed is ensuring for its promoters the cordial support of the leading Citizens of Bristol, and we have no doubt that many people in Cheltenham and neighbourhood will take advantage of the facilities which will be arranged by the Excursion Department of the Exhibition for visiting the Exhibition next year."

HOW THE EXHIBITION WAS ORGANISED

Until it was reported in the press, the scope of the Exhibition had not really been appreciated. Now, 12 months before it was due to open, the genie was out of the bottle – there would be no going back. Or would there?

With the publicity campaign underway, and the exhibition site secured, attention now turned to the organisation and the management of the project. The infrastructure put in place was vast and comprised Patrons, a General Council and several Local Committees as well as the Officers already listed.

The Patrons – whose role was to provide support and encouragement, and potentially some funding, numbered more than 60 people and included all the Mayors and all the Chairmen of the district councils in the West of England and South Wales. Other 'champions' of the exhibition included 16 Members of Parliament, 5 Earls, 2 Lords, 2 Bishops, 2 Archdeacons, 5 Reverends, and 4 Sirs. Although most of these gentlemen didn't have strong Bristol connections, two former Sheriffs of Bristol, the President of the Bristol Teachers Association and, just for good measure, the City Coroner were also listed as Patrons.

The General Council – another influential group 'including some of the leading people of the day' - provided credibility and gravitas to the functions that they oversaw:

Education – Sir Isambard Owen, Vice Chancellor of Bristol University

Science and Electricity – Prof Sylvanus Thompson, Professor of Physics, Finsbury College

Sports, Games and Physical Culture – Lord Desborough, President of the 1908 Olympic Games

Civil Engineering – Prof Cawthorne Unwin, President of the Institute of Civil Engineers

Transportation – The Rt Hon Viscount Churchill, Chairman of the Great Western Railway, 1908 to 1934

Agriculture – James Sykes Gamble Esq, Botanist and Fellow of the Royal Society

Chemical Industries – Sir Thomas Boverton Redwood Bt, Chemist and Petroleum Consultant

Various Industries – W Herbert Singer, Proprietor of J W Singer, Art Metal Workers, Frome

Decorative Art and Furnishing – W H Spindler, MD of Newbery & Spindler, house furnishers, Bristol

Social Economy – Sir Edward O'Malley, Lawyer and Judge and Attorney General to British Colonies

Colonies – Sir John A Cockburn, former Premier of South Australia

Colonies - Col Sir Henry M Pellatt, Founder of the Toronto Electric Light Company, Canada

Army – Field Marshall Lord Methuen, career soldier, Boer War veteran and former Governor of Natal

Machinery – Capt H Riall Sankey, Engineer, Designer & Director of Marconi Wireless Telegraph Co Ltd

Machinery - Mark Robinson Esq

Finally, on the organisational front, several local committees and councils were established to oversee the detailed arrangements for the various attractions, competitions and events:

Fine Arts Committee

Music Committee

Sports Committee

Pageant Honorary Council

Pageant General Committee and a

Fur and Feather Committee

Nearly 200 local people served on these Committees and now that they were in place and making their plans, the publicity machinery got into gear again during the summer of 1913. The press updated their readerships with the latest news, with the Exeter and Plymouth Gazette on 15th August 1913 giving plenty of detail…

"BRISTOL EXHIBITION
MUSIC AND SPORTS
MONEY PRIZES FOR CHOIRS

◆

The summer season of 1914 will have for one of its principal attractions the Bristol International Exhibition, to be held from May to October. We have already outlined the general scheme of the Exhibition, which will be held upon a charming site, almost beneath the Clifton Suspension Bridge. The grounds will laid out in quite gala style, and flower-decked gardens and beautiful buildings will join in making a scene of much attractiveness, and the light and joyous side of the Exhibition will be as pronounced in character as the educational and commercial.

The educational side has been largely developed in the last few weeks, and a rough outline of the programme of Music Competitions is now available. The Exhibition will open upon 11th May and thenceforward until its close, there will be a constant succession of interesting daily events.

The first big Music Competition will be on 3rd June, when choirs of 200 mixed voices will be heard in some of the most impressive music that can be selected, and the prizes will range from £150 downwards. On the following day there will be a competition for choirs not exceeding 40 female voices. The 6th June will be Brotherhood Day at

which, amongst other features, there will be music contests for which upwards of £100 in prizes will be offered and it is anticipated that members of the Brotherhood from all over the Kingdom will attend.

On 17th and 18th of June there will be contests for male voice choirs of 60 and 80 members, as well as for string quartets, solo violin, violoncello, and pianoforte, and a large number of prizes will range each day from £30. On the 20th June, children will hold the platform, and will compete as village choirs, school string bands, and in folk songs and Morris dances. On 1st July there will be competitions open to the United Kingdom for male voice choirs of 200 members, the prizes ranging from £150. On the 2nd July there will be competitions for Church and chapel choirs, and on the 4th for the National Sunday School union.

The larger musical festivals will be continued on the 15th and 16th July, the former day being devoted to South Wales and Monmouthshire the 16th to the English counties excluding Monmouthshire. On each of these days £230 will be distributed in prizes, male and mixed voice choirs both competing. On the 18th there will be competitions for public schools, a most interesting event including Children's Societies for 50 girl and 50 boy voices, the prizes ranging from £20.

These are the Principal items of the music programme, but in addition thereto the 29th August will witness a great Brass Band Contest, bands coming for competition from all parts of the United Kingdom. In connection with these events, it will interest our readers to know that the Adjudicators include such eminent musicians as:—Sir Edward Elgar, Dr Walford Davies, Dr W C McNaught, Dr Frank Merrick, Dr A. J. Silver, Prof Granville Bantock,

Mr. Harry Evans, Mr. Hans Wesseley, Mr Cecil Sharp, Mr Daniel Price, Mr John Acton and others.

The sports' meetings will be opened upon the 16th May, the second taking place on Whit-Monday, 1st June, when the West of England Championships will be brought off and upon the 25th July and 4th August other great sports' meetings will be held. On all these occasions championships will be competed for, as well as the eliminating trials for the Olympic Sports. Upon the 26th September the events of this section will reach their climax in the great Marathon race, which will be terminated in the sports grounds of the Exhibition. The prizes in all the events will be upon a handsome scale and will attract competitors from all parts of the United Kingdom and the Continent, as well as from some of our Colonies. Included also in the sports section will be frequent physical culture displays of a highly educational order.

Empire Day will be celebrated at the Exhibition upon the 23rd May, because the day itself will fall upon Sunday, and the demonstration will include a combined parade of Territorials, Boy Scouts, and National Reserves and a spectacular review of the same, a feature of the proceedings being the participation therein of contingents of Overseas Dominions Cadets.

The great feature of the Exhibition, the historical Pageant of Bristol and the West, will be inaugurated upon the 18th June, when the first dress rehearsal will be held. To this an invitation will be sent to all Infirmaries and Hospitals in Bristol and South Wales, and arrangements will be made for such patients as can attend to travel with every care and consideration for their comfort. The second dress rehearsal of the Pageant will take place upon the following day, and invitations will be extended to thousands of school children of Bristol to witness the performance. The Pageant proper will commence upon Saturday, 20th June, and it will proceed every evening until the 4th July, although it is probable that its popularity will lead to its continuance for a further period.

The week commencing 27 July will provide a series of exciting Fire Brigade demonstrations, the National Fire Brigades Union organising some elaborate competitions, for which drafts from most of the Brigades throughout the West of England and South Wales, as well as from France and Belgium, will assist in giving highly interesting manoeuvres, the proceedings concluding each evening with magnificent displays of fireworks. From this period onward there will be firework displays every Wednesday and Saturday evenings, and military tattoos, always a most popular feature, are being arranged for every Saturday. The general scheme also includes exhibitions for roses, sweet peas, poultry, birds, dogs, and cats; and dates will be set apart for the benefit of the Lord Mayor's Hospital Fund, and a great parade of decorated motorcars and cycles, and a flower carnival, and, more attractive than all, an Actor's Day, in which all the leading actors and actresses of London have promised to take part and produce special plays for the benefit King George's Actors' Pension Fund.

We may conclude by observing that the programmes of music, sports, and other competitions which we have briefly reviewed are still being formulated by the various Committees of ladies and gentlemen of Bristol and the Western Counties, and active work is being pushed forward in the determination to make the events in every way successful."

PAGEANT PLANNING

Once the press had reported on the general scheme of the exhibition and on the musical and sports events in particular, it went pretty quiet on the publicity front. However, beavering away in the background was the Pageant Master, who, along with Miss Blanche Beatrice Barber, had set up a Pageant Office at Edgecumbe House, Richmond Hill, Clifton by the end of 1913. The rent payable was £175 per annum.

John Henderson, described in the press as one of the 'greatest Masters of Pageant in the World' had spent nearly 30 years producing grand spectacular effects, and had practical experience of pretty much every kind of theatrical production both indoor and outdoor. This was to be Henderson's twentieth pageant and he and Leolyn Hart worked on dozens of projects together. Henderson had also spent part of every year engaged on productions in Canada and the United States as well as in the UK.

Henderson was meticulous in his planning. Of his work in Bristol, Henderson said *"None of this is fancy work, everything is accurate. The stirring events of the city's history lend themselves admirably to re-enactment. This will be the last word in Pageants…."*

For months, Henderson consulted old books, photographs, documents and maps; he scoured the British Museum and other museums and libraries and visited the places in Bristol that were to provide the inspiration and historical backdrop for his 'Pageant of Bristol and the West'.

His idea was to portray Bristol's history through a Prologue, three Epochs and an Epilogue. The epochs were to cover three distinct periods – 875 to 1373; 1486 to 1663 and 1764 to 1831. Each of these would be divided

John Henderson studying his models in the Pageant Office in Clifton.

into a series of Episodes and the entire production would comprise 14 scenes and last for two hours.

Henderson turned his study at Pageant House into a model-makers studio. He reproduced his ideas by making scale models of each of the theatrical structures and scenery effects. The models were made in cork and painstakingly painted to replicate the actual effects he wished to show.

Once he was clear on the stories he wished to tell, his next task was to recruit an experienced theatre team to help him run the pageant and to recruit 1,200 local volunteers to perform in the show. He'd get cracking on this once the finances had been secured.

THE FUNDING OF THE EXHIBITION

Unlike the Festival of Empire in 1911 that was funded by the Government, the Bristol International Exhibition was an entirely privately funded, commercial venture. Early funding for preliminary costs of around £5-£10,000 was by way of debenture loans provided in agreements with George Parfitt, Consulting Electrical Engineer from Keynsham and one of the exhibition company directors; the Westminster Building and Construction Company Ltd from London, (the lead contractor) and Arthur Collins, J Ernest Hawkins, Thomas Hill, and Edmund Francis Trump.

The exhibition's bankers were the Wilts and Dorset Bank in Bristol.

As the start date of the exhibition got closer, the organisers put in place a number of Guarantee Funds to raise the capital they needed. Fund 'A' was for £20,000 and was raised by Directors of the company and their friends; Fund 'B' was also for £20,000 and was underwritten with the help of William Tyson, a London-based specialist Financial Agent.

The third Fund, known as the London Guarantee Fund, was for £80,000. This fund was underwritten by Lloyds of London and many 'names' including tea brokers, metal brokers and merchants all supported the venture. Most of the fundraising agreements were signed during March 1913 but only formally registered a matter of days before the exhibition opened.

The exhibition company took out insurance to guarantee exhibition receipts from all sources to the tune of £95,000 – but this was only payable if the exhibition continued until at least 10th October 1914.

The prospectus for the Guarantee Funds listed all the Patrons, the General Council and all the Officers involved in the project and set out expected revenues and expenditures:

REVENUE

Space Lettings, Concessions and Refreshments	£85,101
Gate Admissions (based on two million visitors)	£76,500
Share Capital	£2,240
Amusements and Attractions	£22,961
Total	£186,882

EXPENDITURE

Administration	£33,487
Buildings, Roads and General Construction	£59,000
Entertainments, Grants to Fine Arts, Sports, Music, Pageants etc.	£17,129
Lighting & Power, Insurances, Advertising, Land Rents & Taxes, Railway alterations	£31,350
Total	£145,966

The estimated net profit was £40,916. Assuming this would be realised, the organisers undertook to devote the profit to:

- Repayment to shareholders of the capital value of their shares plus 5% interest for two years
- The balance divided into three portions:
- 20% to the charities of Bristol and South Wales
- 40% to shareholders
- 40% to the Guarantors, subject to stipulations

In today's money (2014 prices), the expected revenue was £15.1 million, the forecast expenditure £11.8 million and the estimated net profit, a handsome £3.3 million – a margin of 22%.

BRISTOL TO BRISTOL IN 207 DAYS

With much of the background activity for the exhibition completed - apart from any sign of construction work - elsewhere in Bristol another seemingly more important commercial venture (at least in Bristol's eyes) got underway.

As 1913 gave way to 1914, Henry Riseley, or 'Mr Bristol', embarked on an around the world voyage to Australia, New Zealand and Canada. Buoyed by the success of the Royal Agricultural Show and the connections made with traders, agents and suppliers, the objective was to bring about increased trade between Britain and the Overseas Dominions through the Port of Bristol.

With a relatively new dock at its disposal (the Royal Edward Dock was opened in 1908) and fierce competition for port trade with the likes of London and Liverpool, Riseley was accompanied by Manning Lewis who was the Commercial Superintendent of the Port of Bristol. Lewis knew all there was to know about the advantages of the Port of Bristol and Riseley was a consummate advocate for Bristol and an accomplished international relationship-builder to boot.

Bristol's Trade Ambassadors – as they were known - left for foreign parts on 31st December 1913. They also took in the United States on their mission and by the time they returned to Bristol some seven months later, they had clocked up more than 32,000 miles.

Their first stop was at Perth in Western Australia. They stayed here for two weeks, addressed the local Chambers of Commerce and met with the Farmers' and Settlers' Union and Fruit Growers Associations – all the time, presenting the case for using the Port of Bristol for bringing cargoes into Britain. Whilst in Perth, Riseley and Lewis established a Society of Bristolians in Western Australia and in no time, over 100 Bristol settlers had joined the Society – apparently all keen to help generate trade for the Port of Bristol.

This pattern was repeated across Australia with visits to Adelaide in South Australia, Melbourne in Victoria, Hobart and Launceston on Tasmania (where connections made at the Royal Agricultural Show were renewed), Sydney in New South Wales, and Brisbane in Queensland.

Next stop was New Zealand with visits and presentations in Auckland, Wellington and Dunedin. Common threads coming out of the visits to both Australia and New Zealand were that steamship capacity and frequency of sailings was an issue to and from Britain; the costs of landing cargoes at London were more expensive than the combined cost of landing in Bristol and transporting to the metropolis, and the substantial progress made by German shipping companies in winning trade in Australia and New Zealand and as a consequence, the threat to Britain's traditional trading links.

From Wellington, it took three weeks to arrive in the United States and Canada from where Riseley and Lewis then called on traders, civic leaders and chambers of commerce in San Francisco, Tacoma, Seattle, Victoria, Vancouver, Toronto, Montreal, Boston, New York, Philadelphia and Baltimore, before sailing from Montreal by the St Lawrence route for Bristol.

They arrived back in Bristol on 26th July 1914. The world they had just travelled around was about to change for ever and the city they returned to was being transformed…

A FEAT OF CONSTRUCTION

Before construction work for the Bristol International Exhibition could really get underway, there was a pause in proceedings. Funding and acquiring sufficient labour and materials were the main hold-ups. People who had been in the vicinity of the site at Ashton Gate, had noticed that things had come to a standstill during the early part of 1914 and some doubted whether the exhibition would ever get off the ground.

To dispel these concerns, Leolyn Hart called a special meeting of those interested in the Exhibition and the Pageant on 17th February 1914 at Dunlop's Restaurant, St. Stephen's Street, Bristol. According to Hart's statement, there was now no doubt that Bristol would have the exhibition, and that there would be no lack of energy and enthusiasm to make it a success. He went on to say that the money was now guaranteed. It was the first definite announcement to that effect that he had been able to make, because the arrangements had only been completed during the last twenty-four hours. The buildings would be proceeded with at once…

It was in fact another month before construction work started in earnest, and start in earnest it did. The Westminster Construction Company Ltd only arrived on site nine weeks before the exhibition was due to open and over the following eight weeks, an average of 2,000 workers per week were employed on the site. In one particular week, over 3,000 workmen were engaged on site. All available Bristol carpenters, plasterers, bricklayers and general labourers had been engaged and extra workers were brought in from South Wales and other parts of the West Country. They lodged across the city – bringing valuable money into Bristolian's coffers – and the average weekly wage bill for construction workers was around £4,200. On Saturday 29th May alone, £2,960 was spent on workmen's wages. The Westminster Construction Company had plenty of experience of large scale projects. In 1906 they worked on the Milan International Exhibition and in 1908 they were called-in by the King of Italy to help provide temporary living accommodation following the Messina Earthquake. Also in 1908, they worked on the Franco-British Exhibition at Shepherd's Bush in London and in 1913 they were the lead contractor for the Liverpool Exhibition.

In April 1914, and around a month after construction work had started, journalists were given a tour of the site and handed a location plan showing where all the attractions would be positioned. The sheer scale and scope of the operation was brought home as the huge plaster-cast structures began to take shape. F W Rogers and Co of Bangor Wharf in Cumberland Road, Bristol did very nicely out of the exhibition and supplied much of the pumice concrete and white plaster partitions used throughout the construction.

The term 'White City', used for the area near Shepherd's Bush in London that was the site of the Franco-British Exhibition six years earlier, was also

A group of construction workers, some with their tools, in a pose for the camera.

coined for the Bristol International Exhibition for the first time in this Western Daily Press account on 18th April 1914…

"INTERNATIONAL EXHIBITION IN BRISTOL PROGRESS OF THE PREPARATIONS

◆

Those who have lately passed along Ashton Avenue cannot fail to have been impressed by the extensive preparations for Bristol's International Exhibition. First, public interest was aroused by a maze of skeleton timber erections, brought into existence with wonderful rapidity, and now, in certain places, the constructional work has been carried further, and the name "White City" suggested, the bright sunlight is reflected by the material with which the timber framework is being clothed.

It is an interesting spectacle to watch the preparations for an enterprise of this nature. Bristol has had many industrial exhibitions, but, in area and scope, that now being prepared for in the Rownham Fields promises to be far larger than anything of the kind previously seen in this city, or, indeed, in the West of England. The site has several advantages. On the east side of it Ashton Avenue is the boundary, and thus there is a magnificent approach road both from the city, via the Swing Bridge, and from Bedminster and Somerset from Ashton Road. The enclosure lies between two tramway routes, and a penny fare takes the traveller close to the ground. On the west the boundary is formed by the railway to Portishead, and the exhibition, therefore has two stations already in existence right on its doors. One is the Ashton Gate platform, constructed several years ago to deal with football traffic; the other the Clifton Bridge Station.

There is not much danger predicting that the Great Western Railway Company (possibly by arrangement with the Midland and other companies also) will run excursion

25

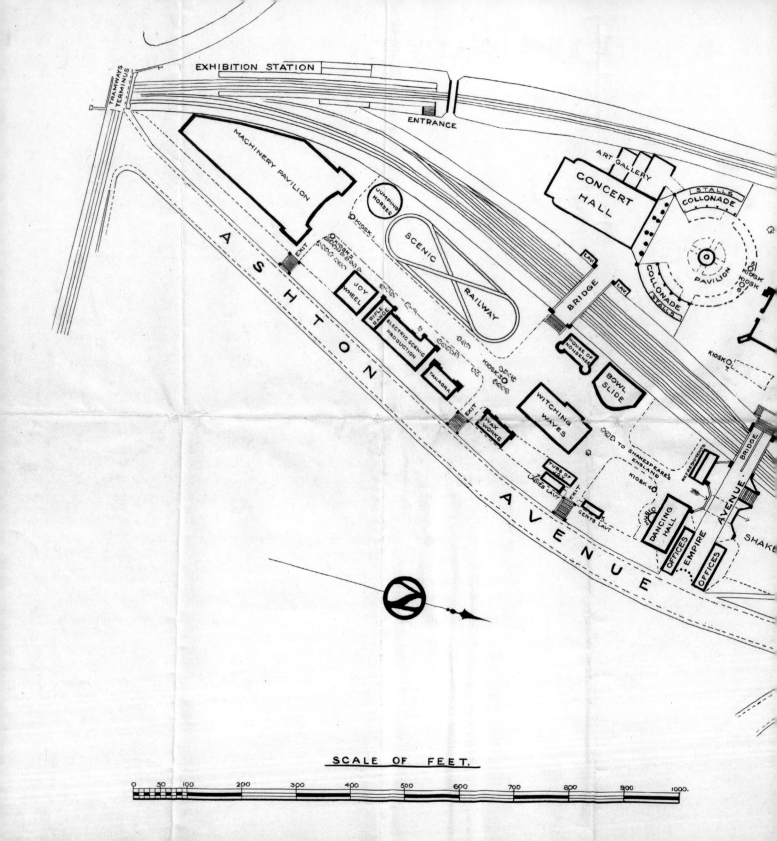

EXHIBITION STATION

TRAMWAYS TERMINUS

ENTRANCE

MACHINERY PAVILION

JUMPING HORSES

SCENIC RAILWAY

KIOSK 1

KIOSK 2

A S H T O N

JOY WHEEL

RIFLE RANGE

ELECTRIC SCENIC PRODUCTION

TANAGRA

KIOSK 30

EXIT

EXIT

WAX WORKS

WITCHING WAVES

TUBE OF JOY

LADIES LAV.T

GENTS LAV.T

EXIT

A V E N U E

ART GALLERY

CONCERT HALL

STALLS COLLONADE

PAVILION

COLLONADE STALLS

KIOSK 106

KIOSK 107

BRIDGE

LAV.

LAV.

HOUSE OF NONSENSE

BOWL SLIDE

TO SHAKESPEARE'S ENGLAND

KIOSK 40

REFRESHMENTS

DANCING HALL

OFFICES

EMPIRE

OFFICES

AVENUE

BRIDGE

SHAKE

SCALE OF FEET.

0   50   100   200   300   400   500   600   700   800   900   1000.

BRISTOL INTERNATIONAL EXHIBITION 1914.

PLAN

SUBJECT TO REVISION.

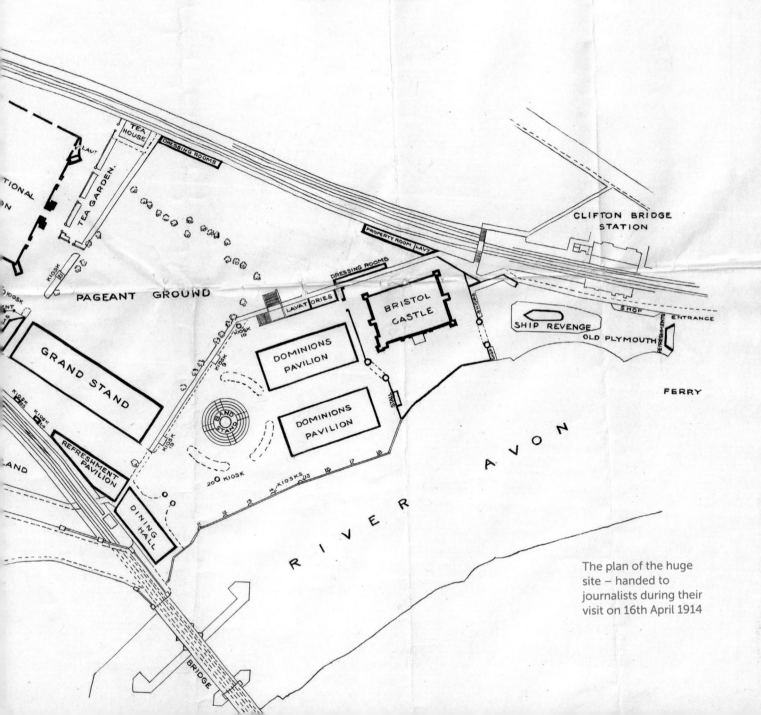

The plan of the huge site – handed to journalists during their visit on 16th April 1914

Clifton Bridge Station. Perfectly located to bring materials and visitors to the site.

trains into one of these stations, and their passengers will be able to pass straight into the exhibition enclosure. To the south the site impinges on Ashton main road by the railway bridge on which the Bedminster electric cars complete their journey; to the north the area extends to the tidal river.

The site is said to be about 40 acres in extent, and it gives room for many buildings and special features, while still leaving large uncovered pieces of greensward. The situation, is not only accessible but is picturesque. The Suspension Bridge and Avon Gorge are seen from the enclosure, immediately to the west of which are the Leigh Woods. Its position convenient also for excursionists brought by Messrs Campbell's steamships, and is anticipated that thousands of visitors from the Principality will reach the exhibition pleasantly and cheaply by water. These facilities may also be extended to popular resorts in Somerset and Devon. Naturally the ground is fairly level, but in places depressions have been filled and made suitable to play a useful part in the design, and considerable work of this nature has been carried out on the bank of the river in the zone where the meadow used to be invaded by high tides. The level has been raised six or eight feet on the river side boundary, and there has

The Egyptian Gardens and Pavilion under construction and The Colonnade with its bright hieroglyphic columns.

been a suggestion that kiosks shall be placed at intervals along this new-made ground fringing the stream. Citizens familiar with the Rownham Fields are aware that they are divided longitudinally by the lines of the Great Western Railway taking this route to the city docks, while in the other direction the area is intersected by the footpath from Ashton Avenue towards Clifton Bridge Station. The fact that railway sidings are in the ground will facilitate the transit of exhibits, and especially those of the heavier order. This dividing railway will be crossed by temporary bridges. The principal of these will communicate from the Empire Avenue, which commences at the main entrance to the Exhibition, and the bridge, like the Avenue of which it forms part, will be completely enclosed, so that the visitor will find himself within the Exhibition grounds.

Having passed over the railway without knowing of its existence; and when he is within he will find huge flights of scenery screening the railway from view. Of this scenery something like three miles is being prepared for the general enclosure and decoration of the Exhibition site. The process of construction of exhibition buildings is fascinating to those who take an interest in mechanical arts. First, there appear the ground lines of stout vertical posts, and soon these are connected by bracings, aiding their stability. Then, as if by magic, the vertical lines are connected by a series of bold semi-circular spans composed of stout planks, shaped and connected so as to form arches. Above these come the rafters and the roof, and while these operations are proceeding, men are seen working on many parts of this skeleton, some of them in elevated positions

The Dominions Building. One of the workers, George Gray, perched on scaffolding in the middle of this image, sent this postcard to Mrs Green in Southampton whilst lodging at 23 Friezewood Road, Southville. He said "I am still roaming. No going home on bike from here. Bristol is a fine place and there is plenty of life here."

where less experienced hands might develop nerves.

In due course the enclosed and arched-over area forms a spacious court, and a pavilion may consist of several of such courts. Next, the open ends of the arched buildings receive attention, and, possibly, while the work is proceeding, other operatives are busy giving to the side of the framework its exterior covering. This is ordinarily done-by fixing to the wooden supports great rectangular slabs composed chiefly of plaster of Paris toughened by fibrous material. These slabs are about an inch thick; at

the edges they fix closely together, and are of such nature that they can be secured to the timbering by flat-headed nails. In the concert pavilion where the work is in a more advanced state than elsewhere, the framework is covered inside and out in this way, and the term 'White City' is a natural one to apply to a group of edifices built on this system. The same fibrous plaster is extensively used for decorative purposes. A design can be easily repeated by the use of a properly shaped mould.

One of the industries now being carried on in

The International Pavilion showing the white plasterboard panels being delivered to site by horse and cart. Another card sent by George Gray – a few days before the exhibition opened - and this time to Mrs Green's daughter, Hilda!

Rownham Meadows is the production of these plaster mouldings, and examples are noticed of the wonderful adaptability of the plan. A visitor sees a short way off what might pass for the marble base of a huge ornamental pedestal, and closer inspection reveals the fact that it is but another form of the plaster work, carefully shaped and strengthened with a kind of coarse texture canvas introduced into the plastic substance. The preparation of these ornamental mouldings is carried out by skilled workmen in the large pavilion that some time hence will

be a concert room accommodating about 5,000 persons. In the same department a huge female figure is being modelled of clay to play some part in the coming show. When sketched by our artist it was not complete, and the wooden framework of the arms and legs had yet to receive the limbs to which it acts as support. The effigy, approximately, will be fifteen feet in height. Of these there will be four perched upon the summit of the International Pavilion, the central feature of the Exhibition.

The larger of our illustrations shows the stage

Rownham Ferry passengers with the Dominions Building and Bristol Castle under construction in the background.

reached in the construction of Bristol Castle on *Thursday afternoon [16th April 1914].* The embattled wall, of which the "masonry" appears to be nearly complete, faces the tidal river, but stands some distance back from it. The constructional procedure is on the principle already described. The covering in this case, instead of being of plain white slabs, is moulded so as to bear a resemblance to boldly chiselled stone work, and in some of the features

of the building where this modelled work is thicker than the thin sheets used for ordinary purposes, clay from the Avon bank has been utilised with fibre for giving additional substance. When the make-believe masonry is fixed in position, any interstices are filled up and then the decorator comes to the scene with tints applied by a brush, and the fortress exterior is complete.

The design of the once famous stronghold, demolished

Bristol Castle six weeks before the Exhibition opened.

A Loxton sketch of the International Pavilion.

by order of Oliver Cromwell, includes arrow-holes produced quite easily in one piece by this convenient moulding method. In skeleton form the fortress could be seen to be composed of two arched courts side by side; the photograph shows the Eastern end of the courts with a network of timber carried across the formerly open spans. Another picture, taken perhaps a week hence, would give, in place of this woodwork, 'masonry' harmonising with the embattled wall.

Within the Bristol Castle it is intended to bring together a loan collection of relics of the Navy and Army, and a special London committee (one member of which is the Keeper of the King's Armoury) and of which Earl Roberts is the chairman, is engaged in securing exhibits for this section. The Castle is at the end of the ground near Clifton Bridge Station, and between it and the pathway through the meadows are several large connected pavilions in

which, according to arrangements, it is expected there will be an interesting display made by Overseas Dominions. The plan of this river-side portion of the site also shows the allocation of a space for a bandstand, and at the northern extremity for a representation of Sir Richard Grenville's famous ship the Revenge.

To the south of the path already alluded to is a large area fringed by tall trees. This is marked out as the Pageant Ground, and here Mr John Henderson, after much study of local records, is preparing for the presentation of a series of episodes partly emblematical but chiefly historical. The Grand Stand, the construction of which has just commenced, will seat over 4,000 persons. Beneath it accommodation will be made for booking-offices, general post office for the public, and a Custom House store, for the Exhibition has been given the status of a Bonded Store for the avoidance of the unnecessary payment of duty on

The impressive reproduction of Shakespeare's England – nearing completion.

SHAKESPEARE'S ENGLAND, BRISTOL INTERNATIONAL EXHIBITION.

articles intended only for exhibition.

The large Concert Hall already spoken of is situated not far from the Ashton Gate Station; and the great structure involving quite a forest of timber, between it and the Pageant Ground, is the International Pavilion. This important department is yet in its early stage, but a great many men are at work on it and it will not be long before the contractors have invested the open framework with the architectural character the architect has designed for it. The centre part of the framework is a tower carried well above surrounding structures, the total height of the building, when completed, being twice the height of the huge Tobacco Stores adjacent to the grounds, and in the courts, of which will be the centre, it is expected that a large variety of English and foreign exhibits will be displayed.

There are other features of this part of the ground planned, but as yet in an embryonic condition, and among them the Egyptian colonnade, which will form the entrance to the Concert Pavilion. Apart from the entrance buildings and connected structures, most of the area fronting Ashton Avenue is still uncovered. Exactly how it will be treated remains to be seen, but a plan, recently issued but subject to revision, allots a large space to a pavilion for machinery motion; another piece of ground to a scenic railway; a third to 'Shakespeare's England,' and neighbouring plots to a variety of sideshows customarily forming part of enterprises of this character.

May 28 is the opening day, and much has to be done in the six weeks' interval. The exhibition ground accordingly presents a spectacle of great activity, and many artisans are employed.

Electric lighting will necessarily form an important feature in the arrangements, and cable is being laid from

The International Pavilion. Almost finished.

the main generating station at Avonbank to the ground to supply the current required. Besides the busy scene in the Rownham fields, the organisation of an exhibition such as this involves much work in other directions, some of it in London and other departments in this city, but these aspects for the present must be left to the reader's imagination..."

The provision of electricity to the site was a massive and expensive undertaking. The Exhibition Company signed a contract with the Bristol Corporation Electricity Department in which the Department agreed to lay two special mains for supplying the necessary current from its Avonbank Generating Station in St. Philip's to the exhibition site at Ashton Gate. Mr Newman, the Cables Superintendent at the Electricity Department was in charge of the operation.

The project involved pulling up about two and a half miles of road and the laying of over five miles of cable. The route taken was along Feeder Road, Cumberland Road, crossing the River Avon at Bathurst Lock, and again at the Swing Bridge at Ashton Avenue. To carry the cable under the river, divers were employed, and this was regarded as a remarkable feat. Most of the under-river work was completed when the tide was out, but occasionally the divers had to continue their work against the incoming tide. Sometimes, there was not enough time to allow the somewhat erratic Avon to interfere with the operations.

The divers were able to dig the trench by hand for the most part, but a steam grab was used for the stretch continuously under water. Once the trench was dug in the bed of the river, the mains were then laid and anchored down by means of chains and iron, and the trench was then allowed to fill up naturally with silt. The cables were capable of dealing with a supply of current almost as much as that required by a city the size of Bath. A new sub-station was built and it comprised nine large static transformers for transforming the extra high tension current to a suitable voltage for distribution to several special buildings in the Exhibition, both for lighting and power.

The supply of electricity for the Exhibition was also used to permanently benefit a large district of Bristol. Certain thoroughfares had electric street lighting provided for the first time.

The Exhibition Company gave the Electricity Department a guarantee over the consumption of at least £6,000 worth of current on the site, and the Department spent around £8,000 on laying the new cables. The outlay on the scheme and the large consumption of current for which the Exhibition gave a guarantee was intended to make a very substantial contribution towards the city's rates.

The illumination of the grounds was to be one of the striking features of the Exhibition. The huge pavilions were to be outlined with electric glow lamps, in addition to the general scheme of lighting in the Exhibition avenues.

With construction work well underway, 300 of the workmen employed on the site were entertained at a smoking concert held on Thursday 30th April 1914 at the Rising Sun Hotel at Ashton Gate. The proceeds from admission to the concert were handed to the fund for the wives and children of the London builders' labourers who were on strike at the time.

THE OPENING CEREMONY

28th May 1914 was a busy day. At mid-day and ahead of the scheduled 2.30pm opening ceremony, publicity manager William Jones, entertained a large group of journalists from London, South Wales, Bristol and adjacent counties.

The majority of the newspaper men saw the preparations for the first time, and to some, "strangers to this district, the lovely view the Avon Gorge and the Suspension Bridge, obtainable from the enclosure came as a pleasing revelation". Many others to whom the local scenery was not unknown expressed surprise at the extent of the enterprise that in the previous two months had been carried almost to completion point. The remark, "I had no idea anything on this scale was

DOMINIONS' PAVILION & BANDSTAND.
BRISTOL INTERNATIONAL EXHIBITION.

Bandstand, Dominions Pavilion and in the distance, Old Plymouth.

intended," illustrated the kind of impression that the first glance conveyed to the minds of not a few of the journalists.

Although much had been achieved over the previous eight weeks, it was apparent that many finishing touches remained to be given to the buildings, and still more to the display of the exhibits for which they were intended. Nonetheless, the press party enjoyed their tour of the exhibition site and afterwards were entertained over lunch in a Dining Room overlooking the Dominions

Gardens.

After lunch there were several speeches and William Jones was master of ceremonies. After the King's health was toasted, he thanked Mr T E Hawkins, representing the contractors for the work they had done so far. Hawkins took the opportunity of talking about some of the other exhibitions he'd been in involved with and how, normally, his company would be given more time to complete construction work. He also had no doubt that the Exhibition should have been more largely supported

The Illuminations.   Bristol International Exhibition.

BURGESS & CO., BRISTOL. COPYRIGHT.

8

One of a series of postcards showing the exhibition buildings illuminated by night – thanks to the efforts of George Parfitt and his team of electricians.

by Bristol people – a veiled criticism aimed at the city's civic leaders and its movers and shakers. However he felt certain that, overall, Bristol wished the enterprise to succeed and that they were going to receive the support of the citizens.

Bristol's attitude to the exhibition was also mentioned in the next speech by Bristol journalist, Mr G F Stone, who responded on behalf of the provincial press. He remarked that an exhibition on the scale now being arranged, and a pageant illustrating events in local history, had long been overdue in Bristol. It had been left very largely to others to shoulder the financial responsibilities involved in undertaking these twin enterprises, but Bristolians could not free themselves from the duty of making, as

far as possible, the resulting Exhibition a success. The city's credit in this matter was at stake, and it was much to be desired that an effort, begun in so spirited a fashion, should be heartily supported by Bristol people, so that the expectations formed with regard to it might be fully realised.

Stone's speech further highlighted the ambivalence Bristol showed towards the exhibition. Six years later Stone would go on to co-write 'Bristol and the Great War'.

Lord Mayor Swaish and the Lady Mayoress arrived on site shortly after 2.30pm and were accompanied by other city council representatives and the Mayors of Wells, Malmesbury, Tewkesbury and Chippenham. With pipers from the Scots Guards playing in the background, the civic party made its way to the Concert Hall for the opening ceremony where they were greeted by Leolyn Hart.

Hart thanked Lord Mayor Swaish for attending to open the exhibition and apologised for its incomplete state, but marvelled at the progress made in a little under eight weeks on site. He said he'd heard that Bristol loved music, and music would be one of the greatest features of the exhibition. He then passed over to Lord Mayor Swaish to formally open the exhibition. Before Swaish could say a word, a woman dressed in a mauve hat and white coat and skirt, jumped to her feet near to the orchestra and shouted, "They are torturing women in prison". She went on to say "I call on all women…." But before she could finish, the suffragette was ushered from the building.

After a short speech, during which Lord Mayor Swaish made a slightly barbed comment along the lines, 'if we could get behind the secret imagination of the people preparing the exhibition we will probably find this to be one of the greatest shows on earth…' he declared the exhibition open.

The afternoon attractions comprised a series of inaugural musical concerts featuring the Bristol Symphony Orchestra and in the evening a choir of 450 voices

A rare souvenir from the Exhibition thought to have been made in West Africa. Note the spelling error. (PHOTO: DAVID EMENEY)

sang many songs in the Concert Hall. There were a few teething troubles with the electrics, but George Parfitt from Keynsham and his team of electricians were on hand to put things right. As it turned to dusk, the mass of visitors marvelled at the sight of the illuminated buildings and the opening day was concluded with a firework display held in the pageant ground and organised by Messrs Pain & Co – pyrotechnic artists from London.

Although unfinished, the exhibition was now well and truly open…

EXHIBITION ATTRACTIONS

Visitors entered the exhibition from Ashton Avenue, and after paying their admission fee of one shilling for adults (half price for children), came straight into **EMPIRE AVENUE** – designed to be a bright and colourful series of artistic impressions, painted on canvas and illustrating various beauty spots in the Empire. The first being Rhodesia, where the methods of irrigating and cultivating soil were depicted; the next was India that was suggested by an example of an Indian Bazaar, inhabited by natives and selling the wares of the Empire. In this area was also a large painted view of the Taj Mahal. Australia was illustrated by showing foliage and vegetation of the 'Never never' land by a reproduction

BRISTOL INTERNATIONAL EXHIBITION 1914

DAILY PROGRAMME

VIRTUTE ET INDUSTRIA

PRICE: TWOPENCE

Leaving Empire Avenue, the visitor would have passed over a newly constructed steel bridge and would now come face to face with **THE INTERNATIONAL PAVILION** – a massive and spacious building, 150 feet high and a floor space of 65,000 square feet. The building was surmounted by four large symbolical figures, bearing a huge globe on their shoulders. Inside the Pavilion was an exhibition of manufacturing featuring many leading commercial organisations and showing recent advances in industrial life.

Passing out of the Pavilion, the visitor entered **THE EGYPTIAN GARDENS** – surrounded by a large Colonnade with massive columns modelled with hieroglyphic and other Egyptian ornaments. Within the Colonnade there was a building modelled on Egyptian architecture that served as a refreshment kiosk, and surrounding it were lawns and floral displays where visitors could sit, relax and take in the surroundings.

A covered walkway led to the **PAVILION OF MUSIC** which was capable of seating 4,000 people and an orchestra that could also accommodate a choir of 1,200 voices. The centre of the building comprised

of Burgoyne's vineyards of Australia, with figures representing workmen gathering grapes and by expanses of orchards with those on one side of the Avenue in blossom and on the other bearing fruit. Another section represented Malaysia and was devoted to rubber cultivation and showed various methods of tapping trees, with natives at work.

A good opening day's attendance.

a huge wooden floor made from Canadian satin wood. The Souvenir Programme to the exhibition suggested that here, visitors could indulge in their devotion to Terpsichore, ie their delight of dancing. Close to the Pavilion was the Exhibition Station of the Great Western Railway that would bring thousands of visitors from Wales and the West of England.

From the Concert Hall the visitor crossed another large steel bridge over the railway and entered the

PLEASURE SIDE OF THE EXHIBITION.

Here, there were plenty of thrills and spills for the enjoyment of young and old:

There was a **FIGURE EIGHT ROLLER COASTER**, built at break-neck pace, that gave visitors a thrill over a one-mile roller-coaster track and nearby was

BOSTOCK'S ARENA AND JUNGLE that apparently proved very popular when it appeared at the Festival of Empire at Crystal Palace in 1911. It was also

The loan collection of mainly military objects on show inside Bristol Castle.

one of the great attractions for amusement seekers when in did seven consecutive seasons at Luna Park on Coney Island in New York. In the Bristol exhibition, the Jungle was open to the public all day and was designed to be a lesson in biology as well as fun. In the Arena, with its lion shows, performances took place four times daily.

THE BOWL SLIDE was designed to provide a 'hearty laugh and a fascinating sight to the looker-on'

THE CRAZY KITCHEN was where visitors could – if so inclined – 'break up plates in the happy home'

THE RIFLE RANGE was no ordinary shooting gallery. It consisted of 'life targets' with images of leaping and running animals projected on a target using the latest cinematography techniques, so that the 'sportsman' could fire at figures in their natural surroundings, and finally

THE HOUSE OF NONSENSE with its series of mirrors and other features was designed to send the visitor away 'delighted and in a happy mood'.

There were other amusements/entertainments

FIGURE EIGHT COASTER.
BRISTOL INTERNATIONAL EXHIBITION.

Photo by Knighton & Cutts. 23

Figure-Eight Coaster, or Scenic Railway, a new attraction for Bristol thrill-seekers. England's first was in Blackpool in 1907.

on show including Lilith – the Flying Lady and a demonstration of dog skills by Major Richardson, a well-known dog enthusiast and breeder. In the late 1890s, Richardson began breeding and training dogs – mostly Airedales – for use by the armies across Europe and they were particularly highly valued by the Germans, Spaniards, Turks, Italians and Russians. When the First World War broke out, Germany had 6,000 trained dogs, Britain had just one Airedale.

Immediately prior to the Bristol International Exhibition, Richardson was in Russia and helped at trials that were training 300 dogs for army, police and railway duties. In England, Richardson's dogs helped to locate missing people/casualties and were used to track down criminals on the run. At Bristol, Richardson's dogs were wearing Red Cross arm bands.

During the First World War, Richardson was eventually drafted-in to help the war effort. The War Office secured his services in 1916 and he set up a Dog Training School that supplied dogs to the Western Front

The Village Green where visitors could buy toys, sweets, brushes and brooms and have their palms read.

for use as messengers and ammunition carriers…

Moving away from the main amusement area, visitors passed under an Old English archway and entered **SHAKESPEARE'S ENGLAND**, described as 'an oasis of delightful old-world architecture', surrounded by scenery depicting Shakespeare country. This section contained an exact replica of Shakespeare's reputed birthplace in Stratford-on-Avon; a Village Hostelry with light refreshments; Shakespeare's Library where books relating to the Bard could be examined and bought; a Tudor House furnished with examples of early English furniture and kitted-out by Oetzmann & Co of London; and the Village Green where continuous performances of Folk and Morris dancing took place as well as occasional dances by the pipers of several Scottish regiments.

Shakespeare's England was designed and created by Jennie Cornwallis-West – Winston Churchill's mother - who was also behind the Shakespeare's England exhibition at Earl's Court in 1912. It was not a resounding success with the New York Times describing it thus, 'So far, from the pecuniary point of view, the show has been an unmitigated failure…'

Cornwallis-West's financial track record with the Earl's Court exhibition didn't appear to put off the organisers of the Bristol International Exhibition who went out of their way to secure her services for the Bristol version of 'Shakespeare's England'. A contract was signed between Cornwallis-West and the Exhibition Company in April 1913 that provided for a £1,000 payment to Cornwallis-West, payable in four equal instalments

Bandstand and Australian Pavilion. Bristol International Exhibition.

Spirella Hall, sponsored by the company that made women's corsets, where mannequins wore the fashions of the day.

"SHAKESPEARE'S ENGLAND." Photo by Knighton & Cutts, 28

Shakespeare's England including a replica of Anne Hathaway's Cottage, netted Jennie Cornwallis-West a tidy sum.

"BRISTOL CASTLE". BRISTOL INTERNATIONAL EXHIBITION. Photo by Knighton & Cutts 25

The outside of Bristol Castle. Not the original demolished in 1656, but the 1914 replica variety. (AUTHOR'S COLLECTION)

of £250. The first payment was made in May 1913, the second in January 1914, the third was due seven days after the exhibition opened with the final payment on 1st July 1914. In addition, Cornwallis-West was due to receive 0.5% of the gross gate receipts from entry to the exhibition and 10% of the gross revenues from all the side shows, space lettings, amusements and entertainments.

By way of further remuneration, Cornwallis-West was also allotted 200 fully paid up shares in the Exhibition Company and just for good measure she was provided with a First Class railway season ticket from London to Bristol and return that was valid from 1st April to 31st October 1914.

Adjacent to Shakespeare's England were the **DOMINIONS GARDENS** that were laid out deliberately to take in the views of the Suspension Bridge and the Avon Gorge. The River Terrace was laid out with lawns and flower beds. The nearby **SUNKEN BANDSTAND**

KE'S FLAGSHIP "REVENGE".

STOL INTERNATIONAL EXHIBITION,

Photo by Knighton & Cutts, 40,

The '*Revenge*' would have been quite a sight for boating and other traffic coming up the Portway.

would, throughout the season, feature the music of many famous bands of the King's Army.

Within the Gardens was also the **DOMINIONS PAVILION**. Inside, the building contained exhibits provided by the Australian Government and it had a **CHEMISTRY** section providing 'intellectual treats' and much amusement and frequent 'lecturettes' with demonstrations and experiments. A large space was also devoted to a **FINE ART GALLERY** that displayed over 1,000 paintings and was described as 'the largest and most interesting that has ever been displayed in the West of England'. Another part of the Pavilion was devoted to a cosy bijou theatre where 20 mannequins displayed and wore the latest fashions of the day. This area also included a range of exhibition cases containing examples 'of all that is most interesting to women-folk in dress and fashion'.

Adjacent to the Pavilion, the visitor would find an

THE EASTERN TEA GARDENS.
BRISTOL INTERNATIONAL EXHIBITION.

Photo by Knighton & Cutts. 41.

The Tea Shop at the Eastern Tea Gardens with tea-room staff in the garden and spectacular scenery effects to the right. The space behind is the home of Bedminster Cricket Club.

apparent faithful reproduction of **BRISTOL CASTLE**. The architects of the exhibition had studied 'national depositaries of ancient documents' and by doing so had been able to reconstruct the castle with 'considerable fidelity so that it can be said that the building before us is as nearly as possible a replica…' Inside Bristol Castle was a display of **NAVAL AND MILITARY RELICS** put together by a London Committee headed by Lord Roberts. The displays included a collection deposited by the King and Queen of souvenirs received by them during a tour of the Dominions and from a visit to India.

Passing from Bristol Castle, the visitor crossed a moat and entered **OLD PLYMOUTH** with an old quay-side inn, quaint shops and timbered houses and a makeshift harbour that would contain a full-size replica of **DRAKE'S *REVENGE***. Sailors dressed in period uniform were to act as guides for visitors. The ship wasn't completed until 3rd July. Visitors then passed

The first letter from the Exhibition Ground was believed to have been sent on 25th May 1914 – three days before the opening ceremony.

The construction of the *'Revenge'* was only completed in July 1914 – shortly before the exhibition closed.

to the west side of the Dominions pavilion, through the Dominions Gardens and arrived at the **PAGEANT GROUND**. When the Pageant performances had ended, the Pageant Ground was intended to be used for Championship Athletic Meetings, Military Tattoos, Firework Carnivals and Fire Brigade Contests. A stand capable of seating an audience of 1,000 people was on one side of the ground and beneath it contained a **POST OFFICE** where Exhibition Postcards containing an official Exhibition post-mark could be sent.

Moving on from the Pageant Ground, one of the prettiest spots of the Exhibition was **THE EASTERN TEA GARDENS**. At the edge of the site with Bedminster Cricket Club opposite, the gardens were flanked by canvas tapestries adorned with tropical scenes and foliage and floral displays. Teas and cakes were available inside and in the gardens.

A key feature of the Exhibition was **THE NIGHT PICTURE**, where the river terraces, the broad avenues, the flower beds and lawns and all the Exhibition pavilions were outlined with myriads of lights and pyrotechnic effects.

Despite all the glitz and the glamour and the undoubted spectacle in South Bristol, the finances of the Exhibition Company were not in good shape. It really did appear to have over-extended itself to a massive degree.

EXHIBITION GOES INTO RECEIVERSHIP

After only eight days of operation, on Saturday 6th June 1914, Leolyn Hart shut the exhibition and rumours were rife that it would stay closed. 500 workmen, who were due on-site to continue the construction work were laid off and other staff and visitors wishing to get in were locked-out. A notice was posted on the entrance...

"Owing to want of funds, no men will be put on today". The same fate befell another 400 workmen who turned up the following day. As the workmen collected their tools and as stall-holders and show proprietors gathered in groups discussing the situation, it was hoped that funds might yet be found to carry on the exhibition successfully. Leolyn Hart was less optimistic.

The initial capital of £100,000 had been exhausted and in an interview with the Western Daily Press, Hart was critical of Bristol's attitude and said it was futile to expect any significant monies to be raised locally to keep the enterprise open. He went on to ask… "Was it too much to hope when Bristol had so materially benefited, that Bristol people should now come forward and ensure a successful continuance of the venture?"

The closure of the exhibition appeared to trigger a clause in three agreements between the Exhibition Company and the Debenture Holders that left them little choice but to put the Exhibition Company in the hands of a Receiver. They wished the exhibition to continue until its scheduled end date of 14th October 1914 and in order to secure their interests they appointed Arthur Collins, Chartered Accountant from Bristol as Receiver and Manager. He took up his role first thing on Monday 8th June and found a cash balance of £25 19s 4d in the Exhibition coffers. The shock caused by the exhibition closing spurred some local gentlemen to come forward with offers of financial support, to keep it open and to ensure that the Pageant of Bristol could proceed. Arthur Collins issued a statement to say that he was negotiating with a likely party to provide the funds (thought to be around £25,000) for the whole exhibition to be carried on as originally intended. Encouragingly, after four days of closure, the exhibition re-opened on Wednesday 10th June. Although attendances were low, on the bill that day included a concert by the Victoria College Glee Club from the University of Toronto, freshly arrived at Avonmouth on the liner Royal George.

The exhibition limped on until the end of the week when on Saturday 13th June 1914, Arthur Collins sent a telegram from London to the offices of the Western Daily Press. It read, "Financial arrangements have just been completed which will enable the original intentions regarding the Bristol International Exhibition to be carried out in the entirety."

Immediately on securing the future funding of the exhibition, Arthur Collins was stood down from his role as Receiver and Manager in favour of Joint Receivers who were named as Joseph Sedgwick of Derby and Arthur Sudbury of London. Leolyn Hart, now much more buoyant, stated in the press that the construction work and completion of the gardens would now re-start and in an effort to boost attendance, the admission price after 6pm would reduce from one shilling to sixpence. Apart from about a week's delay to the start of the Pageant, the rest of the programme for the exhibition should continue as planned, until its scheduled closure in mid-October.

Over the following days there were several changes to the management structure for the exhibition including the appointment of a Mr E H Morgan – of W H Smith & Sons – as Chairman of a Special Committee of Concessionaires, Exhibitors and Stall-holders. John Bellham, the Space and Concessions Director, was nowhere to be seen. Morgan's task was to let the remaining spaces for exhibitors and concessions in the various pavilions. Morgan bought his experience of working on the recent Earls Court,

A selection of the souvenir postcards hastily produced by W H Smith in an effort to improve revenues at the Exhibition.

Dublin and the Franco-British exhibitions to the Bristol site. He was also behind the introduction of a series of 15 postcards specially produced as souvenirs for visitors to the exhibition – printed by who else, but W H Smith.

In an interview with the press, Morgan commented on the management changes and he too was critical of Bristol's attitude and support for the Exhibition, "I think the Bristol Exhibition has the makings of a good Exhibition in it now that fresh blood has been introduced into the management. I think it will be an enormous pity if the Exhibition, having once been started, is not a success. Moreover, it is impossible for Bristol to avoid certain very definite responsibilities in connection with the venture, and under existing auspices I feel that the citizens and the prominent people of Bristol will. I am bound to say that while it is a great pity the Exhibition was not started under stronger auspices, now that more money has been found to complete it, it is hoped that it may end in being a credit to the city.

Morgan went on to say that "having once named the Exhibition 'The Bristol International Exhibition', although it might be unfortunate, and particularly in view, of the fact that a large number of influential people supported it in its commencement, it wasn't possible to eradicate the impression that it was not a Bristol enterprise."

Despite the reprieve, all was not well among the secured and unsecured creditors. There was a feeling that the debenture holders held all the aces and that other creditors were being disadvantaged.

The British Fram Construction Company from Mountain Ash in Glamorgan, one of the sub-contractors and one of the creditors, submitted a Winding Up order on behalf of some of the creditors that was heard by the Bristol County Court on Friday 26th June 1914. In view of the potential upturn in the Exhibition's affairs and the proximity of the Pageant of Bristol – due to run from 29th June to 11th July 1914 - other creditors asked the Judge to adjourn the hearing until 17th July. The Judge agreed to the adjournment.

THE PAGEANT OF BRISTOL

With the financial problems temporarily put to one side, the way was clear for the staging of one of the biggest and grandest outdoor events the city had ever seen. In the two months before the Pageant all 1,200 local volunteer performers attended rehearsals – sometimes 2-3 days a week - on the lawns of 'Pageant House' on Richmond Hill where they were also fitted out with their costumes. The house resembled a clothing factory with seamstresses at work for months. The volunteers were each given a leaflet that explained 'how to be a performer' and they were expected to purchase or at least make a contribution towards the cost of their costumes.

Although John Henderson invented, wrote and produced the Pageant, he had a large team to help him stage the show in addition to the volunteer performers. He had a General Stage Manager in Bertram C Wynn and four Stage Managers – J L Coggins, A C Gildon, John Exton and Arthur Gilmore.

John Wilson of the Oxfordshire Hussars conducted the band and the music was arranged and composed by Carl Hamlin. Bristol barrister and songwriter, Fred Weatherly, wrote the words for the Prelude to the Pageant, along with many of the songs that were sung during the performances. The bands of the Royal Engineers and the

Royal Army Medical Corp played at each show.

Special costumes and wigs were provided by William Clarkson, costumier and perruquier to His Majesty the King; horses were supplied by Messrs Norris, Hardwell, and Cornish; and an old style coach was loaned by J Tuller & Co, Coachbuilders.

A few days before the Pageant started, John Henderson led the cast through the streets of Bedminster

PROLOGUE:

The ancient Brythonic site of Caer Oder, 350 BC to 43 AD, with Druid Temple.
Death of King Donawallo.
The Druid Sacrifice.
Roman Invasion.
Introduction of Christianity

EPOCH THE FIRST: 875 AD TO 1373 AD

EPISODE 1
Caedma the Goatherd's Hut
The Days of King Alfred the Great
The Fight for the Standard and defeat of the Danes

EPISODE 2
The Alwarde Gate, Brightstone
The Quarrel of Lord Brictric with King William I

EPISODE 3
The Robber Barons
Fitzroy and the Rescue of Lady Mabel Fitzhaymo
Death of the Ape Man

EPISODE 4
The Alwarde Gate of Bristow
How King Henry finds a Daughter-in-Law in Lady Fitzhaymo

EPISODE 5
St John's Gate and Ancient Quay
Riot of the 'Cockit Tax' Burgesses and Soldiers

Queen Elizabeth, played by Mildred B Clark, performs her royal duty in Episode 8.

Cromwellian Soldiers performing in Episode 10.

Edward III's Proclamation of Bristowe 'a County'

EPOCH TWO: 1486 AD TO 1663 AD
EPISODE 6
St John's Gate and Old Quay
The visit of King Henry VII
Knights at Tournay and the Sailing of the Cabots

EPISODE 7
St John's Gate and City Cross
By Night

The Plague
The surprise visit of King Henry VIII

EPISODE 8
The Joyous Visit of Good Queen Bess to Bristowe, 1575
Drill of the Famous Harquebusiers

EPISODE 9
The Newgate of Bristole and the Castle, 1645
The Days of the Civil War
The Siege of Bristole
The Treachery of the Mayor's Wife

EPISODE 10
The Newgate and City Cross in 1663
The Restoration and Visit of King Charles II

EPOCH THREE: 1764 AD TO 1831 AD
EPISODE 11
Queen's Square, Bristol, 1764
The Days of Chatterton and Edmund Burke

EPISODE 12
Queen's Square 1831
The Bristol Riots and Burning of the Square
Charge of the Dragoons
Firing on the Mob

EPILOGUE:
A Woodland near Bristol, 1914
Grand Ensemble of all the Pageant and Finale

The Prologue Finale featuring Brythonic Women, Druid Priests and Caradoc Warriors.

to help drum up interest. The opening evening of The Pageant was held on Monday 29th June 1914. It lasted two hours and was made up of a series of scenes.

The Pageant was popular and very well received in the press, but not as well attended as Henderson would have liked. However, it was extended by a further week until Saturday 18th July 1914 and did what John Henderson intended it to do, "…to rehabilitate the Exhibition". Although audiences were close to the 4,000 capacity for the final few night's performances, Henderson accepted that the Pageant wouldn't recover its initial expenditure. He was quite bitter about the support received within the city and at a performers celebration following the last show on 18th July he let his feelings be known,

"The apathy of the people of Bristol in this has been wonderful. Here we have 1,200 citizens of Bristol who have given months of their time and their petty cash to do this thing, and what do we find —first week, nil; second week, very little. And it is only through the kindness of the Press that they have become alive to the fact that they have really a show on this ground."

He added that the people of Bristol ought to have shown a greater appreciation. The Lord Mayor, he said, had shown his appreciation, and when he attended the other night he expressed in no doubtful terms his full appreciation of the Pageant, and said that he had never seen a show like it. After expressing the hope that the Pageant would live long in their memories, he said that he had travelled a good way through the world, and had "done" something like 28 or 29 of these spectacular shows, but he could tell them that he would never want for a better set of boys and girls than he'd had in Bristol…

Around 175 'Empire Girls' pose for the camera at the end of the Grand Finale.

EXHIBITION COMPANY WOUND-UP

As the curtain came down on the final performance of the Pageant of Bristol, the Exhibition Company too was about to perform its last act. The Winding-Up hearing adjourned until 17th July was re-convened and the petition re-submitted. The Bristol County Court was packed with legal teams representing the Exhibition Company, the Debenture Holders and the Creditors.

Judge Gurner heard how the Exhibition Company had been formed in 1912. It was not a Bristol company but one exploited from London, and the Exhibition had been rather thrust upon the city. There was much discussion in court as to the rights of the debenture holders and the unsecured creditors and into the probity and legality of some of the financial instruments put in place by the Exhibition Company and its advisers. Hot foot from the Pageant, Fred Weatherly donned his barristers wig as counsel for a group of creditors who wished the Exhibition to remain open and were opposed to the Petition. He argued in favour of keeping the exhibition running until its scheduled end in October, as he believed this to be the best way of achieving some recompense for his clients and other creditors.

Having heard the submissions from respective Counsel's, Judge Gurner adjourned the hearing until Monday 20th July 1914 when the legal teams and the press again filled the Court. After listening to more submissions, Judge Gurner concluded that as far as he could see, the Exhibition Company was insolvent from its inception and he saw no reason to suspend the order. In his view the Company was a non-entity, the only entity being the debenture holders. He ordered the Exhibition Company be wound-up but stressed that didn't imply that the exhibition would be closed. The Official Receiver of the Court was appointed Provisional Liquidator and Joseph Sedgwick, receiver for the debenture holders, told the press that he had effectively been running the Exhibition since 13th June as receiver for the debenture holders and that he would continue to do so. The Exhibition would go on as usual… but not for much longer…

BRISTOL'S TRADE AMBASSADORS RETURN

Less than a week after the Bristol International Exhibition Company had been wound-up, Henry Riseley and Manning Lewis arrived back in Bristol from their trade mission around Britain's Dominions. They arrived back in Bristol on 26th July 1914. The world they had just travelled around was about to change for ever and whilst they were away the Bristol they returned to had seen the rise and spectacular fall of an enterprise that could really have done with Henry Riseley's expert guiding hand.

Riseley would have been just the fellow to oil the civic and commercial wheels and provide a bridge between the ambitions of the exhibition organisers and the reality of operating in a city proud of its independence and traditions but wary of outsiders. Alas, Riseley was not available, and maybe he wouldn't have wished to be involved in a venture that was well meant, but flawed from the outset.

Riseley and Manning Lewis presented a report on their findings firstly to the Lord Mayor on 21st August 1914 – Just eleven days after the start of the war – and then to the Bristol chamber of commerce in October 1914. Since the Exhibition company was wound up attendances to the site had seen a marked increase. Seemingly stung by being criticised for 'petty jealousies' and 'small minded provincialism', maybe, just maybe, Bristol was finally getting behind the Exhibition that carried its name. The improvement was shortived. As soon as war was declared the War Office requisitioned railway and shipping transport. Visitor numbers dried up and the directors and the receiver for the debenture

The exhibition curtain was about to close for good for the Country Dancers and the Funniest Men in the Pageant.

holders had little choice but to close the Exhibition.

A meeting of creditors was held on Monday 10th August and they agreed to ask the Court to appoint a liquidator in place of the Official Receiver. This was agreed by the Court.

The Bristol International Exhibition closed for good at the end of the day on 15th August 1914. The site, that for months had been the scene of so much fun and excitement, at least for Bristol's citizens, would shortly be transformed for a more sombre purpose…

PART 2

WHITE CITY BARRACKS

OUTBREAK OF WAR

With an eye on the changing climate, the Exhibition organisers donated the proceeds from the last day of the Exhibition to the Bristol Branch of the Red Cross and anyone in a Territorial Force uniform was allowed in free of charge. In fact there weren't many 'Terries' left in Bristol by 15th August 1914. The 4th and 6th Gloucesters were already on their way to Danbury and Little Baddow in Essex for further training and to help defend the east coast in case of an invasion; and the Territorial units of the Field Ambulance, the Royal Field Artillery and the Royal Engineers had also left for their war stations. The Regular Forces and Army and Navy Reservists had left Bristol even earlier.

However, there would shortly be other khaki-clad locals who would find excitement, food, comradeship and a roof over their head on the Ashton Meadows site. The troubles of the Bristol International Exhibition were soon forgotten and any city-wide guilt felt at its demise was quickly swept under the civic carpet. The war conveniently allowed the whole affair to be lost from memory and consciousness. Apart from future financial spats, there was no inquest…

THE CALL FOR VOLUNTEERS

More pressing was the need to respond to the newly appointed Secretary of State for War's demand for a New Army of civilian volunteers. Lord Kitchener took prompt steps to expand the army by 500,000 men and on 7th August 1914 his first public appeal for 100,000 men appeared in the press under the heading 'Your King and Country Need You'. His call was for men aged between 19 and 30 to enlist 'for a period of three years or until the War is concluded'.

Bristol's response was not as swift as the War Office would have liked, but that was due, at least in part, to the absence of adequate contingency planning within the military. The infrastructure to cope with the deluge of recruits was not in place.

In pre-war days, recruitment for the Regular Army and Special Reserve in Bristol was carried out at No.8 Colston Street and came under the War Office's Southern Command. The office was staffed by one permanent Recruiting Officer – retired Major John Carr, MBE - with the assistance of three pensioner Recruiting Sergeants – Quarter-Master Sergeant Cook, Colour-Sergeant Clark and Sergeant Thyer. In peacetime it was a relatively low key operation. At the time, around 100 recruits were processed on a daily basis at recruiting centres across the country. A busy day in Bristol would see around 10 recruits wanting to enlist. That was about to change…

On the declaration of War, it soon became apparent that the level of staffing in the Colston Street office was completely inadequate. The morning of 4th August 1914 saw the first batch of potential recruits turn up, but Major Carr was elsewhere. On mobilisation, his orders were to report to Avonmouth as Port Transport Officer in order to co-ordinate arrangements at the Docks - a key embarkation port for much of the mechanical transport for the British Expeditionary Force. This took him away from his peacetime recruitment duties – at least in the short term.

With further local public announcements about the New Army on 9th and 10th August, and even more volunteers trying to enlist, two local retired ex-officers

'Caterpillars' at the bottom of Park Street en-route to Avonmouth – part of the fleet of military haulage vehicles whose embarkation to France was co-ordinated by Major Carr.

stepped in to assist the harassed pensioner recruiters. They were Lt Col W E P Burges who had retired from command of the 3rd (Special Reserve) Battalion, Gloucestershire Regiment the previous October, and Captain W A R Blennerhasset, formerly of the Derbyshire Regiment, who had retired in 1903.

Lt Col Burges opened a separate office in the Old Market area of Bristol for volunteers for the New Army, while the Colston Street office dealt with recruits for the Regular Army and men from specialist trades.

Lord Kitchener was frustrated with the shortcomings of the recruiting system he inherited and appointed Conservative MP Leo Amery to the War Office as unpaid Director of Civilian Recruiting for Southern Command.

Amery was a noted commentator on 'war preparedness' having written extensively on the Boer War for The Times when he covered the campaign as a journalist. Amery's task was to galvanise local efforts and on 11th August he set out to visit the principal towns and cities in the area. By 14th August, he had been to Salisbury, Bristol, Rugby, Coventry, Warwick, Birmingham and Worcester. On his return, he recommended 'a systematic scheme for enlisting public opinion and civilian drive behind recruiting over the whole country'. This philosophy was adopted by the War Office and led to the creation of the Parliamentary Recruiting Committee (PRC) and the growth of the 'Pals' movement at the end of the month.

Amery's visit to Bristol took place 'late in the night'

of 11th August. He called on Lord Mayor Swaish at his home at Willsbridge, and Amery impressed upon Swaish the necessity of organising civilian assistance. Amery was somewhat critical of the complacent attitude he encountered in Bristol but at least found Swaish amenable to his urgings.

BRISTOL CITIZENS RECRUITING COMMITTEE FORMED

The next day the Lord Mayor convened a meeting of senior and influential local figures at the Royal Hotel in the City. The meeting was chaired by Sir Herbert Ashman, a Liberal Councillor, and was also attended by officials from the War Office. The meeting decided to form a committee of citizens to run a large recruiting office and the Bristol Citizens' Recruiting Committee (BCRC) came into being immediately. The BCRC initially comprised 13 members – mostly from the political and mercantile establishments across the City.

The Lord Mayor was elected Chairman, and he deputed his duties to Sir Herbert Ashman. Lt Col Burges was appointed Chief Recruiting Officer for Bristol - a temporary post that gave Major Carr the time he needed to co-ordinate the transportation plans at Avonmouth.

The Colston Hall was chosen as a special recruitment centre and the practical steps were taken to make the building ready for use within a few days. Symbolically, it opened its doors for the first time for would-be recruits at 10am on Saturday 15th August 1914, just as the Bristol International Exhibition was preparing to close its doors for the very last time at the end of the same day.

Postcard designed by Bristol Citizens Recruiting Committee.

The recruitment centre was staffed by voluntary assistants and clerks seconded from local businesses and by 24 former non-commissioned officers who were engaged to take recruits through the enlistment forms and to assist with supervision. Magistrates made themselves available to administer the formal attestation and City Councillor, Dr Barclay Baron of the Bristol Royal Infirmary volunteered to organise the medical services and he secured the help of 20 general practitioners to examine the recruits who were starting to arrive in large numbers.

With the Recruitment Centre now open, the BCRC held its first meeting in the same building on 17th August 1914. Initially, the BCRC met daily at 11.00am and its key early priorities concerned transport, mobility and distribution arrangements for its members, helpers and supplies. Communicating the Committee's deliberations to the press and the general public was also seen as crucial; as was the advertising campaign to attract recruits.

With no immediate funding from the War Office, the

Chairman suggested that a guarantee fund be established to cover the costs of advertising for recruits. Promises of funding to the tune of £143 were received immediately from 19 gentlemen – many of whom were Committee members.

Within the next 24 hours, the wording of posters, placards and advertising postcards had been agreed with Sir Herbert Ashman, suggesting the text and the design for the small advertising postcard. Ashman seized on the mood of the day and used the emotive 'Your King and Country Need You' message contained in the Public Notices issued by the War Office. Rather than use the image of Lord Kitchener, now synonymous with recruiting propaganda from the First World War period, Ashman chose an image of King George V for the postcard. Two Bristol printing companies offered to produce all the advertising materials and one of them; ES & A Robinson & Co got the job to produce 100,000 of the small postcards and offered to provide them at cost price – 4 shillings per 1,000 copies. Within the next 48 hours, 50,000 of the small cards had been printed and delivered to the Colston Hall.

Dunscombe, the Bristol Photographer produced 24 glass plate slides of the postcard design, free of charge, and these were made and delivered in one day to the 24 Picture Houses in Bristol for showing during performances. Proprietors agreed to display the image at least twice per day during film screenings.

Bill posters were made and put up in offices and at other sites across the city and advertising space was reserved in the local newspapers.

Although they might not have been behind the White City Exhibition, over the following two weeks, many of

Posters produced by the Parliamentary Recruiting Committee.

Bristol's civic elite wished to associate themselves with the work of the BCRC. The Committee structure was re-jigged to allow the major tasks to be undertaken by an Executive Committee of around 20 of the more energetic members, with sub-committees to perform specialist functions such as Finance. Those supporters whose assistance was confined to lending prestige or acting as financial backers, became members of a theoretical 'General Committee'. The minutes of the BCRC and its sub-committees chart the thinking and strategies employed by the Committee as its role evolved into what it termed a 'movement' – ie to help establish Lord Kitchener's Second Army.

As well as publicity and advertising, the BCRC organised speakers for outdoor meetings, for addresses delivered from open motorcars and at 'mass rallies' at the Colston Hall and other locations across the City. The measures adopted by the Committee were similar to those used by the political institutions of the day and

Early recruits marching from the Colston Hall.

locally as it saw fit. The publicity, advertising, meetings and rallies attracted nearly 2,000 recruits in the first two weeks of the campaign.

The early recruits, once formally attested, were given a small round lapel badge inscribed 'Bristol Citizens Recruiting Committee' with the word 'ENLISTED' appearing in capitals across the middle. The BCRC felt it was important for new recruits to demonstrate to other civilians that they had volunteered.

it is not surprising that the early members of the BCRC included some of the local political agents representing the main parties. These individuals would later form Bristol's links with the PRC, formed by members of both Houses of Parliament. While encouraging local autonomy and initiative, the PRC intended that constituency party organisations should assist the local recruiting authorities.

The PRC was established 'in order that the grave issues of the war should be fully comprehended by the people and thereby to give a powerful impetus to recruiting'. The PRC commissioned around 200 posters that were mostly aimed at domestic civilian audiences. Most of the posters were published prior to conscription in 1916.

Aided by the national advertising campaign and its own local efforts, the BCRC ploughed-on with recruiting

FORMATION OF 'BRISTOL'S OWN'

The Chairman of the BCRC had been considering an appeal 'in connection with the better class young men of Bristol, appertaining to a Citizens' Battalion'. The thinking was that as Bristol was proud of its commercial history, it was up to 'young businessmen and professional's' to prove themselves worthy of that past by applying for a place in the new battalion. Ashman approached the War Office and a few days later was able to report to the Executive Committee that he had 'secured a telegram from Lord Kitchener sanctioning a scheme whereby a Battalion be formed of better class men of Bristol and District, and that the scheme had already been offered to General Pittcairn, General Officer Commanding Southern Division for his approval'.

On 1st September 1914, the War Office appointed Lt Col Burges to the post of Commanding Officer of the new 'Bristol Battalion'. For a while, Burges combined his recruiting duties with his new role, until Major Carr was in a position to take back control of the Regular Army Recruiting operation.

Burges had substantial military experience. He'd already commanded battalions during a 33-year military career and among his distinctions were the passing of the tactical course for Field Officers and the field artillery course for Infantry Officers. He had also received a Certificate of Distinction from the School of Musketry at Hythe in Kent. These skills were to prove extremely valuable later on…

The BCRC decided that an appeal to the Athletic, Mercantile and Professional young men would be a good heading for any circular or press release, and took immediate steps to contact Banks, Insurance Offices, Merchants, Manufacturers, Retailers and Political, Athletic and Social Clubs. Advertisements appeared in the local press although these omitted the word 'Athletic' and called for unmarried applicants between the ages of 19 and 35 'engaged in mercantile or professional work, but not necessarily a public school man'.

The Western Daily Press on 4th September 1914 noted that *'the mercantile and professional classes have formed but a small percentage of those who have gone.... and now have the means to contribute'*. Application forms for the Battalion were available at the Colston Hall, Bristol Stock Exchange, Commercial Rooms, Constitutional, Liberal and Clifton Clubs and at various banks and insurance company offices. Bristol's desire to raise its own 'Citizen's Battalion' was mirrored across the country and particularly in larger urban and industrialised communities during August and September 1914. Recruiting Committees believed that the prospect of serving together would act as a stimulus to local recruiting, particularly among sections of the population who had a negative perception of army life

Lt Col Burges with his officer cadets.

– often regarded as an 'employer of last resort' - hence Bristol's intention to focus its recruitment on a particular section of society.

Lord Kitchener supported these local initiatives which gave the War Office some breathing space from the problem of providing for more recruits, as the 'Pals' battalions were to be housed, equipped and fed from resources raised by the local civic recruiting committees - until such time as the Army was ready to receive them for Divisional training.

Although no proposals for 'pals' infantry battalions were sanctioned by the War Office after November 1914, 145 Service and 70 Reserve Battalions were raised by civilian recruiting committees. Subsequent appeals were made during 1915 for civilian committees to raise specialist units for technical branches of the army, such as artillery batteries.

From 4th September 1914, recruiting figures reported to the BCRC distinguished between the 'New Battalion' and those for 'Lord Kitchener's Army'. National recruiting reached its highest on 3rd September 1914. In Bristol, it had already peaked by the end of August:

Date	New Army	Bristol Battalion	Total
28th Aug	296	-	296
29th Aug	440	-	440
3rd Sept	396	-	396
4th Sept	304	30	334
5th Sept	196	110	296
7th Sept	188	131	319
8th Sept	291	91	382
9th Sept	141	58	199
10th Sept	82	61	143

The Bristol Battalion was officially titled the '12th (Service) Battalion, Gloucestershire Regiment'. However, it immediately became known as 'Bristol's Own' and the press referred to it as such from mid-September onwards.

Recruiting for 'Bristol's Own' started a little too late to have benefited from the early recruiting boom. Before the battalion was first mooted, recruiting at the Colston Hall was for general service and once this organisation got into its stride, many men who enlisted locally found themselves sent to regiments other than the Gloucesters. The BCRC widened the search for recruits by writing to recruiting centres across the West Country.

The local recruitment drive received a boost when in September, the BCRC received from Fred Weatherly a rousing recruiting song, 'Bravo Bristol!' written specially for the new battalion. Fresh from writing the songs at the Pageant of Bristol and from representing some of the Exhibition's creditors during the Winding-up Petition, Weatherly was at it again and got his friend, Ivor Novello, to set the song to music. They both agreed that the entire proceeds from the sale of the song's sheet music would be given to the Regimental Fund of the Bristol Battalion. The BCRC authorised the £12 cost for engraving and supplying 1,000 copies of the sheet music which was sold around Bristol and the song was performed at various recruitment rallies around the City.

By the middle of September 1914 around 500 recruits to 'Bristol's Own' had volunteered. After the formal experience of enlistment, medical examination and attestation, the recruits' introduction to Army life was relatively gentle. The Colston Hall now doubled as Bristol's Recruiting Centre and the Headquarters of the new battalion. Space was tight, but the first parades took place there during four sessions on 16th September. The recruits paraded in their civilian dress and were commended for 'their quickness and their alert appreciation of orders.' Lt Col Burges had taken the opportunity of selecting experienced NCO's from among the applicants passing through the recruitment office. Some of them had served with Burges before and many had Boer War experience. They helped to establish the new battalion, and to supply the training and know-how necessary to mould it into an effective fighting unit.

Initially billeted at home, the recruits received a 'billeting allowance' of two shillings a day as well as their soldier's daily shilling. At first all that was required of them was to turn up for a daily drill session at the Colston Hall.

BRAVO, BRISTOL!

(Weatherly, Novello - September 1914)

When the stalwart merchant venturers
Set out in days of old
They sailed with a Bristol blessing
To find a land of gold
And now there's a grimmer journey
There's a sterner call today
But the men of Bristol answer
In the good old Bristol way

It's a rough long road we're going
It's a tough long job to do
But as sure as the wind is blowing
We mean to see it through
Who cares how the guns may thunder
Who recks of the sword and flame
We fight for the sake of England
And the honour of Bristol's name

O men and boys of Bristol
You swarm from far and wide
The rich man and the poor man
Thank god, are side by side
March on, our hearts are with you
We know what you will do
The spirit of your fathers
Is alive today in you

It's a rough long road you're going
It's a tough long job to do
But as sure as the wind is blowing
We know you'll see it through
Who cares how the guns may thunder
Who recks of the sword and flame
You fight for the sake of England
And the honour of Bristol's name

And when the seas are free again
And the bloody fields are won
We'll tell our Bristol children
What Bristol men have done
Their deeds shall ring forever
From Avon to the sea
And the sound of the march
of the Bristol men
The song of their sons shall be:-

It's a tough long way we're going
It's a tough long job to do
But, as sure as the tide is flowing
We mean to see it through
Who cares what the victory cost us
We must win it just the same
We fight for the sake of England
And the honour of Bristol's name

Fred Weatherly photographed in around 1913; the words to 'Bravo, Bristol!' and the front cover of the sheet music.

The first battalion strength parade of the new battalion – Artillery Grounds, Whiteladies Road, 22nd September 1914.

The first public showing of the new battalion took place on 21st September 1914. The day started at the Colston Hall where the battalion paraded in front of the Lord Mayor, the BCRC, and a large audience in the public gallery. Instrumental in establishing the BCRC, the Lord Mayor's speech at the event was typically stirring:

".....in the Bristol Battalion are men drawn from the professional and commercial classes, men of education and varied ability, whose services in this great cause will be invaluable. This is the type of man called for by the exacting demands of modern War – men with personality and resource. When battle lines now range over a front of 100 or 200 miles, or even more, it is no longer possible for the supreme commander to exercise direct or immediate control over the swaying fortunes of battle in any particular area. That must be left more and more to individual officers, and individual men, such as I see marshalled before me this morning. And I am quite sure you will do your part, and when you come back we will have another meeting in the Colston Hall to welcome you."

Following his speech and escorted by Lt Col Burges, the Lord Mayor inspected the recruits and was impressed by their smartness and physique. The inspection was followed by a march through the main streets of Bristol that, according to the press reports, were lined with hundreds of enthusiastic and supportive citizens. Now 700 strong, the battalion was very much in the public eye.

As numbers continued to increase, drills were moved

to the Artillery Grounds at Whiteladies Road, Bristol and the very next day - 22nd September - saw the first battalion-strength parade held there.

In these first few weeks, the recruits learnt the basics of marching, turning and formal movement in squads of 50 (ie platoon strength), before progressing to company drill when four platoons would be marshalled together.

The lack of space at the Artillery Grounds made training even a single company very difficult. This was also the case for the company officers, themselves either having to learn the rudiments of parade-ground techniques, or the novel methods of handling what to many of them, would have been 'double companies' from their previous military experience.

Bedding being moved into the Fine Art Gallery. 'B' Bond warehouse is opposite.

EXHIBITION SITE BECOMES A BARRACKS

The Chairman of Bristol City Football Club came forward and offered the stadium and grounds at Ashton Gate for the purpose of drilling and a possible rifle range, helpfully noting that the Club would only need the Stadium on Saturday afternoons! The offer was duly noted by the BCRC as 'should be carefully borne in mind'. However, at its meeting on 14th September it was reported that a few members of the committee had walked around the grounds of the Bristol International Exhibition and that Lt Col Burges had sent a report to the War Office recommending the site be acquired for the use of the new battalion.

The War Office responded along the lines that providing the Committee could raise a battalion, then it should proceed with negotiations with the Receiver of

The inside of Bristol Castle becomes a dormitory.

the Exhibition with a view to acquiring the buildings and the grounds at a maximum rent of £50 a week exclusive of rates and taxes and on the basis of a weekly tenancy. A few days later, a representative of the War Office visited the exhibition site and was impressed with the

Some of the new recruits making themselves at home.

The International Pavilion – now a drill hall and dining hall.

buildings. He confirmed that the Army Council would purchase the buildings – the 30 acre site would remain in the ownership of Great Western Railway and the City Corporation. An entry in the Receiver of the Exhibition's Accounts dated 18th September 1914 shows a payment of £8,100 was received from the War Office for the buildings – around £650,000 in today's money.

By the end of the month all the formalities had been completed and the War Office took over the site and in turn, handed it over to the Royal Engineers and the Army Service Corps in order to make it suitable for use as a barracks.

Although the timber buildings had been intended as temporary structures, by mid-October 1914 they had been adapted as serviceable, if draughty barracks, mess-rooms, drill hall, dining room and officer's quarters. The foul drainage system at the former Exhibition site was not functioning properly and following a squabble between the Sanitary Committee and the Royal Engineers, the

Sanitary Committee carried out the necessary drainage works – leaving the question of payment to a later date.

By the middle of November 1914, the battalion was fully billeted at its new headquarters…

Each company had its own hall for use as a barrack, in which beds were drawn up along the walls; two platoons each side of the room. The former Dominions Pavilion and the replica of Bristol Castle were popular barrack rooms. As friends within each company had, where possible, been allocated to the same platoon – even to the same sections – experience of barrack life was not too bad, although there were differing views. One of the recruits, Harold Hayward, recalled it as 'not dissimilar to conditions at boarding school'. Whereas, Pte Robert Anstey… 'The beds were very uncomfortable. The palliasses were unsafe, because they had the habit of collapsing, particularly when helped by some mischievous individual!'

One of the first priorities was catering. The Clifton

A Fatigue Party set to work next to the 'Revenge'.

Catering Company offered to carry out the feeding of the men, but the BCRC decided to appoint Cox and Co who were the Army Contractors. The contract allowed for the feeding of the men at a cost of 1s 9d per man per day but with a rebate of £15 per 100 men per month. The allowance received from the War Office amounted to 2s 0d per month – so a small profit for the BCRC. This arrangement continued for a few months until sufficient cooks had been enlisted into the battalion and issued with 'cook's whites'. From then on, the battalion bought its own food wholesale. The men were certainly well fed. Breakfast comprised porridge with milk, followed by bacon and eggs, ham, brawn, liver, sausages or kippers –

with plenty of bread and butter and mugs of tea. Lunch comprised roast pork, beef or mutton with Irish stews and lots of fresh vegetables. Desserts included bread, rice, treacle and plum puddings and there was plenty of stewed and fresh fruit to go around. Tea consisted of bread, jam and cake and for night operations, hot soup was generally provided.

When the Battalion moved into the White City Barracks, no rifles or uniforms had been issued to the recruits. The only distinguishing mark which the men carried was a small circular badge worn on the left lapel of their civilian clothing and bearing the legend 'New Bristol Battalion Gloucestershire Regiment'.

Another Fatigue Party in front of the Dominions Pavilion – some are proudly wearing their New Bristol Battalion badges.

TRAINING GETS UNDERWAY

Owing to pre-war spending restrictions at the War Office, the shortage of equipment in 1914 was chronic throughout the New Armies. The lack of uniforms in particular was keenly felt by the recruits and the misgiving that they were not 'proper soldiers' until clad in khaki was widespread. Various expedients were employed to procure at least some sort of uniform for individual units. The most widely adopted was the 'Kitchener blue'

serge, which was ultimately being issued at the rate of 10,000 suits per day.

The War Office allowance for clothing the men in uniforms was £7 5s 0d per man. The BCRC succeeded in placing contracts to fulfil the clothing requirements for £7 0s 10d each. Another small margin.

The infantry rifle of 1914 was the Short Magazine Lee-Enfield MkIII, (SMLE) which had been introduced in 1904. As with

The New Bristol Battalion badge.

72

A route march returning to White City barracks – seen here in Long Ashton in October 1914.

uniforms, existing stocks were just sufficient to equip the Expeditionary Force. Infantry training programmes were heavily dependent on personal arms since all but the most basic elements of drill involved handling the rifle. 'Drill purpose' substitutes were accordingly issued to battalions as early as practicable together with a few modern rifles for demonstration and comparison. While some battalions were issued with wooden dummy rifles, 'Bristol's Own' were provided with around 400 old Lee-Metford weapons which had been obsolete even at the time of the South African War (1899-1902). The benefit of these was that, with bayonets, they were very similar

in length to the SMLE with its longer bayonet. The Lee-Metfords however were not suitable for musketry training.

Although unable to fire their issued rifles, the recruits were taught to judge the distances of targets and the principles at least of handling and firing the SMLE. They grew accustomed to actual shooting at a small-bore range at the White City Barracks which had been constructed at the initiative of Lt Col Burges.

The BCRC also secured the use of the nearby Clifton Rocks rifle range at Hotwells. The subject of musketry was close to Burges's heart and he was intent on doing

On parade in Greville Smyth Park – The Scenic Railway is being demolished in the background.

everything he could to provide the Battalion with the best possible training. Burges was an accomplished shot having attended the Musketry Course at Hythe in 1912. In early training, he conducted the instruction himself.

Around 20 small bore rifles and a large supply of ammunition (around 80,000 rounds) were obtained and the value of this early training became apparent later when, in competition, the battalion gained the best shooting scores in the New Armies. Sgt Arthur Bailey became the champion shot of the entire New Army.

Training was conducted to the syllabus laid out in the 'Infantry Training Manual 1914' that was issued by the War Office in early August 1914. The training regime included route marches, by day and by night, of steadily greater duration with increasing burdens of equipment. The scope for field training was limited to the Ashton Court Estate and the smaller Greville Smyth Park.

Some early experiences of drill and route marches were recalled by a few of the recruits:

PTE EWART HALE

"Rifle drill was tedious. We sloped, trailed, presented, ordered, reversed, wheeled and piled. We did it for hours until we were totally exhausted. Then we did some more. We all wondered how it would help us when we faced the Germans."

PTE RALPH SMITH

"We used to drill in Greville Smyth Park. Skirmishing, rifle drill, guard duty etc. Night marches took place some nights, chiefly the seven mile march around the boundary of Lady Smyth's. We were not allowed to speak, only in a whisper as everything had to be as quiet as possible."

PTE STAN STREETS

"My main memories of training at Ashton were of lots of drill, lots of trench digging and lots of route marches. All very tiring for an office chap like me...."

UNIFORMS ARRIVE

Unlike many of the New Army battalions, 'Bristol's Own' was kitted-out with regulation clothing reasonably quickly by the end of November/early December 1914, and not long after the entire battalion had been accommodated in its newly-adapted Headquarters. Harold Hayward attributed the relatively speedy kitting-out to Lt Col Burges's ability to 'pull strings' at the regimental depot whose command he had relinquished the year before.

The BCRC had also been working hard with local manufacturers to procure enough sets of uniforms to fit-out the entire battalion. Locally made boots (Bristol had a thriving boot and shoe industry at the time) cost 14s 6d per pair and were of excellent quality, all being soaked in castor oil before issue.

PTE WILLIAMS AYRES

"We were very pleased to receive our uniforms in December. Making our way in groups of 30 or 40, firstly to the tailors for measuring and issue and then to the boot makers for fitting of boots. Finally we were issued with our badges; one at the front and a small back-badge at the rear - the only Regiment in the British Army to have a back badge. Some of us obtained extra back badges and had them made into brooches for sweethearts, sisters and mothers."

PTE FREDERICK TAYLOR

"We got our uniforms around December 1914 and were very proud to wear them. I do remember that to start with, the fitting of puttees was a bit of a job."

Maggs in Queens Road were quick off the mark in producing Army Kits for the new recruits.

PTE THOMAS NELMES

"When we finally received our uniforms it was a really proud day for all of us. It felt so good to stand proudly in our uniforms after spending so much time as soldiers in civilian clothes. Unfortunately there was a shortage of 'Gloster' shoulder titles. We didn't get these for quite some time as I remember."

Recruits posing in their new uniforms. Standing on what is now the site of White City allotments.

The newly kitted-out soldiers of 'Bristol's Own' became the target of professional photographers keen to take souvenir snaps for friends and relatives. One such photographer, Mr E C Stevens, of Arley Hill, Bristol - already an accomplished press photographer - was a regular visitor to the Barracks. Given permission to photograph the Battalion, on most Saturdays, Stevens would arrive with his previous week's prints and sell them to the recruits. He'd take more photographs and the cycle would repeat itself the following Saturday. Many of the photographs in this book are thanks to the efforts of E C Stevens. The souvenir postcards produced by W H Smith for the Bristol International Exhibition were re-printed in a souvenir packet that included 11 assorted views of the Battalion's Headquarters and four extra cards – available in a complete set for just 2d.

On 1st October 1914, with the 1,000th recruit being sworn-in the previous day, and the target of four companies being formed, the BCRC agreed to close recruiting for the battalion. By this time it was recognised in Bristol as elsewhere that the recruiting 'boom' was past. The BCRC had scaled down from its programme of daily meetings on 10th September and had closed the temporary Recruiting Office at the Colston Hall on 28th

Training gets serious. Bottom image; how to kill using a bayonet and top left, trench digging practice behind 'Bostock's Jungle'. Top right shows rifle drilling on the former Pageant Ground. The chap with an 'x' above his head is Pte Edward Young. He sent the card to his friend Stanley Baker from Bath... "We are as far as I know having no Christmas leave, otherwise I would try to see you somehow...they don't half put us through it. I shall have quite a history when I see you again..."

Swiss Drill with 'B' Bond Warehouse in the background. Sgt Major Ward VC – a veteran of the Boer War is standing to the right.

September, expecting that the pre-war recruiting office at 8 Colston Street would prove sufficient. This was not the case, so accommodation at The Guildhall, in Broad Street in the City was made available by the City Council. By October, having completed (as they then believed) their task of recruiting for 'Bristol's Own', the BCRC even considered disbandment, but recognising that their responsibilities for the battalion were, as yet, indefinite, decided 'it was necessary that the Committee should be kept in force'.

It appeared that the BCRC, in the absence of contact with the War Office, shared the widespread view held at the time that Lord Kitchener's appeal had now been answered – with men for the first two New Armies having been found.

TRAINING INTENSIFIES

Training continued in earnest at the White City Barracks and along with Drills, Marches, Trench Digging and Rifle practice, particular emphasis was also given to the use of the bayonet. Much time was spent bayoneting bags

Rifle Drill in front of the International Pavilion.

of straw and although given high priority the aim was probably more psychological – to develop aggression and courage and boost morale. The 'discipline' required by bayonet work was thought of as an end in itself. Practical knowledge such as map reading, trench survival, avoiding machine-gun fire and how to deal with an enemy strongpoint were considered secondary.

Around 90% of the battalion had no previous military experience and so Lt Col Burges, among his many other duties, prepared a small booklet that was published by the BCRC, principally for the benefit of 'Bristol's Own'.

The small brown-backed publication, 'HINTS to Non Com Officers and Men of the Gloucestershire Regiment', contained 30 pages of guidance and instruction on:

Discipline, Saluting, Appearance, Fitness, Marches, Cleaning and Care of Rifle, Equipment, Order for Dress, The Bayonet, The Spade, Scouting, Sentries and Night Work, The Battle, and Correspondence.

The booklet also contained an account of past deeds of the Gloucestershire Regiment and a note from Lord Kitchener on the general conduct expected of the soldiers that was reprinted from a message he sent to the British

No.5 Company in front of Bristol Castle, including, kneeling fifth left, Stanley Barnes, the author's grandfather.

Expeditionary Force as it left for the Western Front - all no doubt designed to bolster pride in the Regiment and underpin all the training and instruction the soldiers had been receiving.

Due to the calibre of the men that had joined the battalion, its strength was weakened by dozens who had received Officer Commissions and were posted to other units. The BCRC twice asked the War Office if it could raise a fifth reserve company of 250 men to plug any gaps. At the same time, (November 1914), the two political agents on the BCRC were summoned to a meeting of the PRC in London that was also attended by an official of the Southern Command recruiting office. The official, Col Gretton, was reportedly critical of Bristol's recruiting efforts compared with local initiatives elsewhere in the country. According to figures compiled by the Ministry of National Service, by the end of 1914, and across all possible routes to military service, Bristol produced a total of 10,217 recruits – around 1.5% of the city's population, compared to 29,424 (4.2%) in Cardiff.

Gretton called for more to be done and requested a further 3,000 recruits from the Bristol area. This touched a nerve at the BCRC as the local press – in particular the Bristol Times & Mirror and the Western Daily Press - also carried articles on 19th November 1914 that criticised the BCRC's apparent lethargy in recruitment.

The Church of England Men's Society converted the Eastern Tea Room into a Recreation and Writing Room for the recruits.

Although there might well have been some truth in this, with the BCRC focussing on housing, kitting-out and training the recruits, the upshot was that on 30th November 1914, the War Office sanctioned the formation of a 5th Reserve Company and through advertisements, public notices and recruiting rallies, the BCRC set about securing another 250 recruits. It was not until 17th February 1915 that the Committee reported that 'E' Company was full.

One of the recruits to the new company was the author's grandfather; Private Stanley Barnes enlisted on 9th December 1914. He was a cigarette machinist with WD & HO Wills at the Raleigh Road, Bedminster

New recruits for the Bristol Heavy Batteries line up in front of Bostock's Jungle – now used by the Royal Garrison Artillery units.

Factory. With another 250 recruits needing to be housed, fed, drilled, equipped and trained, the White City Barracks was filling up.

Although Bristol's Own was nominally recruited from a sector which was defined both socially and geographically, there was wide variability within the battalion.

Declared occupations ranged from gardener and footman to solicitor and company director, with an estimated 60% working in professional, commercial or clerical roles and 40% employed in manual or retail occupations. Although predominantly made up of men with Bristol home addresses, there was a healthy minority

drawn from other areas: Somerset provided around 200 recruits, including 80 or so from Weston-super-Mare; the County of Gloucestershire – outside of the Bristol boundary, supplied at least 80 recruits; Wiltshire and Southern England were the homes of another 30 or so; at least 21 came from Wales, 25 from London and the Home Counties, 18 from the Midlands, and the wider South West provided at least another 15 recruits.

Away from the hard physical drill and training, some leisure facilities were provided for the men to relax when not working or on duty. The Church of England Men's Society converted the former Tea Shop in the Eastern Tea Gardens into a Recreation and Writing Room for use by

Members of one of the Bristol Heavy Batteries pose in front of some of the scenery effects for Bostock's Jungle.

the men. Around 400 books were also provided by a Mr E T Morgan, helped by a gift from the Bristol Libraries Committee. Two snooker tables were also provided as were packs of cards, and games of chess, drafts, and dominoes.

NEW UNITS MOVE IN

In January 1915, the War Office issued a circular to municipal authorities asking them to raise artillery units from a list of options. Possibly stung by previous criticism, the BCRC chose to recruit one of the smallest units in personnel – a Heavy Battery and Ammunition Column – that comprised 6 officers, 25 NCO's, 91 gunners, 64 drivers, 2 smiths, 3 wheelwrights, 3 saddlers, and 3 shoeing smiths. The physical standards for recruits were a minimum height of 5' 8" and a chest of 35½". The unit was raised quickly and included a contingent of around 60 Bristol Policemen. It was named the 127th (Bristol) Heavy Battery, Royal Garrison Artillery and was housed in former White City Exhibition buildings adjacent to the barracks occupied by 'Bristol's Own'. The artillery battery shared the dining halls and drill grounds with their infantry colleagues.

Now on a bit of a roll, the BCRC sought and received permission from the War Office to raise a second

Tea time for some members of the Heavy Batteries.

Heavy Battery and within four weeks, had attracted enough recruits to fill the unit. Over half of the unit was made up of policemen, including more Bristol police and a large contingent from the Gloucester force. Named the 129th (Bristol) Heavy Battery, Royal Garrison Artillery, it too moved into the White City site.

The BCRC was also recruiting to the 14th (West of England) Battalion, Gloucestershire Regiment. Formed in April 1915, this was a 'Bantam' unit made up of men who were under the standard

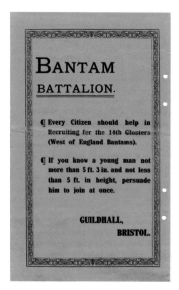

BANTAM
BATTALION.

❡ Every Citizen should help in Recruiting for the 14th Glosters (West of England Bantams).

❡ If you know a young man not more than 5 ft. 3 in. and not less than 5 ft. in height, persuade him to join at once.

GUILDHALL,

BRISTOL.

acceptable height of 5' 3" inches, but above 5 feet. Like the 'pals' battalions, 'bantam' units were a phenomenon of 1914-15. They originated from an initiative by Alfred Bigland, Conservative MP for Birkenhead, and a total of 24 such battalions were raised across the country.

The War Office appointed Major John Carr as Commanding Officer. After co-ordinating regular army recruitment in the city and sorting out transportation arrangements at Avonmouth Docks during early mobilisation, this was Carr's third key role of the war. As the

Some of the 'Bantams' relaxing in front of piles of straw – probably used to feed the increasing number of horses.

'Bantam' battalion moved into the White City Barracks, accommodation got even tighter and space for field training became more limited. Tents were erected and the Bantams and the Heavy Batteries slept under canvas for a while.

'Bristol's Own' had now been in training for over six months. The likelihood of the battalion leaving Bristol for Divisional Training - and hence coming under direct War Office responsibility – got ever closer. In April 1915, 'Bristol's Own' marched out of the White City Barracks in full equipment, a company at a time, to Chipping Sodbury in South Gloucestershire for a week's field work. Using uncultivated land on the Duke of Beaufort's Estate, the Battalion practised setting-up camp, digging rudimentary trenches, erecting barbed wire and removing enemy wire and building fortifications.

During their week at Chipping Sodbury, the men were billeted in threes and fours with local families who, at a time of rising prices (particularly food) were glad to receive them and by all accounts they were treated well.

FAREWELL 'BRISTOL'S OWN'

As the spring of 1915 wore on, it became clear that 'Bristol's Own' would soon be on the move. The possibility was reinforced by the long-overdue issue of SMLE rifles and the arrival of Vickers guns for the Machine-gun Section. Expectation of imminent departure was so high that on

E & F Coys, 12th Glos, Departure.   Bristol 26/6/

'E' and 'F' companies of 'Bristol's Own' leaving the city from Temple Meads and the front cover of the Farewell Programme.

Whit Monday, 24th May 1915, the battalion, accompanied by the 'Bantams' battalion and the two Heavy Artillery Batteries, paraded through the City.

'Bristol's Own' attended a civic Farewell Ceremony the following evening at the Colston Hall, presided over by the Lord Mayor and joined by the recruits' friends and relatives. 'Bravo Bristol' was sung to

FOR KING & COUNTRY.

COLSTON HALL, BRISTOL.
Tuesday, May 25th, 1915.

FAREWELL
CONCERT

12th (Service) Batt. Glos. Regt.
(THE "BRISTOL" BATTALION.)

Chairman:
The Right Hon. THE LORD MAYOR
(Alderman J. SWAISH).

Grand Organ   -   -   Mr. GEORGE RISELEY

send them on their way, but the ceremony was premature - the battalion did not leave Bristol until a month later, on 23rd June 1915. Another reserve company of 250 men ('F' Company) had also been sanctioned by the War Office in early June 1915 and the recruits to this and to the earlier 'E' company would leave Bristol three days later.

The departure of the main body of four

H.B.R.G.A Marching to Barracks. 979

The Heavy Batteries and the Bantams on their way back to their barracks having seen off their 'Bristol's Own' colleagues.

companies took place the day responsibility for the battalion transferred to the War Office. Bristol turned out in force to witness the spectacle of 'their' battalion with rifles at the slope and fixed bayonets, the officers on horseback and led by the band, marching for the last time out of the White City Barracks, via Hotwells Road, the City Centre, Baldwin Street and Victoria Street and then on to Temple Meads Station where two special trains were waiting. The soldiers had quite a send-off as some recalled in later years…

PTE WILLIAM AYRES

"There were masses of people pressing out into the road, barely leaving enough room for our four abreast column to move away. The station incline was packed and orderly marching was not possible. It was all heart-warming to be greeted so boisterously and to be given such a friendly send off."

PTE ARTHUR JONES

"As we marched through the city streets to Temple Meads station, I had packets of sweets and cigarettes, magazines and papers pushed into my hands, and several times was kissed by complete strangers."

L/CPL RALPH SMITH

"The platform was sealed off so that no one could see us off. To everyone's surprise two girls came along asking for 'D' Company. They started asking for me. Both girls lived close to the house I lived in. A brother of one of them worked at Temple Meads and smuggled them in. Both of them kissed me goodbye."

With the main body on their way to Wensleydale in Yorkshire for further training, it was now the turn of the remaining two reserve companies to be off. They travelled to Sutton Coldfield by train from Temple Meads on 26th June 1915, and like their battalion comrades, received a rousing send-off. The Bantam Battalion and the two Bristol Heavy Battery units lined the route to Temple Meads and after the train had departed, these units paraded through the City and returned together to the White City Barracks – with the Bantams taking over the barrack halls vacated by their infantry colleagues.

After further training in Wensleydale and a musketry course at Whitburn near Sunderland, 'Bristol's Own' moved to Codford on Salisbury Plain in August 1915 to complete its period of intensive training. During the month, the battalion was joined by the two reserve companies, fresh from 'catch-up' training at Sutton Coldfield. At nearly 58, Lt Col Burges was too old to lead the battalion into war and on 16th August 1915, the

command was handed over to Lt Col Archer-Shee. The battalion landed at Le Havre in France on 21st November 1915.

Back at the White City Barracks, the comings – and mainly goings – were now coming thick and fast.

FAREWELL BANTAMS AND HEAVY BATTERIES

By the end of Wednesday 25th August 1915, both of the Bristol Heavy Battery units had left the White City Barracks and were on their way for further training. The 129th Battery was ordered to Woolwich and the 127th left for County Durham in the North East. The 129th Heavy Battery went into active service in France in March 1916 and the 127th Heavy Battery followed two months later at the end of May 1916. The horses that they trained and rode at the White City Barracks went with them to the Western Front.

Saturday 28th August 1915 saw the Bantam Battalion exit the White City Barracks for the last time. The battalion of around 900 officers and men travelled to Salisbury Plain for further intensive training before landing at Le Havre on 30th January 1916.

The four units raised by the Bristol Citizens Recruiting Committee had all left their White City headquarters by the end of August 1915. It had been a frenetic year of recruiting and training and the Barracks became strangely quiet – but not for long. The War Office had invested a significant sum in converting the Exhibition site and buildings into a useful, albeit, temporary facility. Bristol was well-located for military purposes and the barracks was in constant use throughout the war. A

Officers on horseback. The barracks was utilised throughout the war by a succession of artillery and infantry units.

succession of infantry and artillery units made the most of the facilities for varying periods.

One short-term visitor was Guthrie Watson-Williams. An ex-Clifton College student, he'd joined the Officer Training Corps at Bristol University and was seconded to the 3rd Gloucestershire Royal Field Artillery (RFA) based at Whiteladies Road. A contingent of 250 men left Bristol at the end of July 1915 and for a while were based at a camp near Didcot in Oxfordshire where

Watson-Williams became a Second Lieutenant.

In a memoir, he recalled a visit to the White City Barracks…

"We were instructed to collect 200 horses at Avonmouth Dock, just arrived from Argentina, good stuff but as wild as they make, never having had a shoe on or been in a harness, and rather averse to traffic. We boxed to Didcot from which the six mile journey by road was something of a nightmare, especially as our team included very few

who knew one end of a horse from the other. And so our training progressed, slowly maybe, but in good spirits. With the approach of winter (1915) we were ordered to strike camp and march to Bristol, which we did with overnight stops at Newbury and Chippenham, entering Bristol at Brislington Hill, at the foot of which was the tram terminus. Our horses had never seen a tram, and didn't like them, but we fetched up eventually at our target which was the White City Exhibition at Ashton Gate. By then it was raining and nearly dark, with a powerful south west wind, so that the large notice on the tower of the central building caused some misgiving, as it read 'Not to be used in windy weather'.

However, nothing else offered, so in we went, and soon horses were tethered and groomed and fed, and then the men also. I was allotted Ann Hathaway's Cottage in 'Shakespeare's England', and while my batman made up the camp bed I foolishly leant against the wall, which being of canvas and rotten at that, parted in the middle and I found myself in four inches of slushy mud. Of course, to be back in Bristol was grand for me, but I think Mother's housekeeping bills must have soared...

Gertrude Alice Knott – a White City Laundress.

As Watson-Williams was getting his mother to clean his soiled garments, laundresses like Gertrude Alice Knott were hard at work at the White City Barracks trying to keep bedding and soldiers outfits clean for the succession of units passing through.

Gertrude Knott worked at the White City Barracks from 1915 and like so many of her generation kept an autograph book. Every now and again, particularly around Christmas time, she took it to work and got a few of the soldiers to jot down their names and write a poem or a rhyme. The entries show how the Barracks was used by different Siege Batteries and infantry battalions during the course of the war.

Edward Bond was just 10 when he said goodbye to his uncle, Private Francis Bond, when 'Bristol's Own' left the city in June 1915.

"My father and I wanted to see my uncle off at Temple Meads. Before he set off, he gave me his 'swagger' stick with the Gloucesters crest at the top. That was the last time we saw him. He was killed in action on the 21st July 1916 on the Somme."

The same fate befell hundreds of Private Bond's contemporaries. The Somme Battles in particular were a

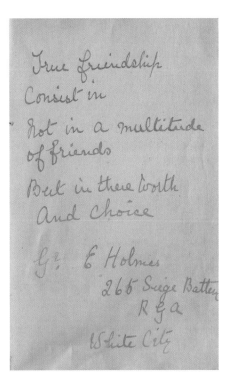

Some of the entries from Gertrude's autograph book.

watershed for 'Bristol's Own'. Of the 950 members of the battalion who fought in the Somme Battles in July and September 1916, 736 became casualties – either wounded, killed or missing.

The battalion was continuously topped-up with drafts of new men from any location and 'Bristol's Own', effectively became 'Anybody's Own'. By early October 1918 and six weeks before the Armistice, the battalion had ceased to be a viable unit and 'Bristol's Own' was disbanded in Velu Wood near the village of Havrincourt in France. Only around 10% of the original members of the battalion were there at the end and the final death toll for the battalion, including around 330 of its original

members, was 765 men.

Among the 'Bantams' battalion 371 men were killed. It was also disbanded in France and 12 officers and 250 men were transferred to the 13th Gloucesters in February 1918. The 127th Heavy Battery lost 24 men, and a similar number were killed in the 129th Heavy Battery.

None of the units raised by the Bristol Citizens Recruiting Committee would ever return to their White City Barracks and around 500 of the men who responded to the Committee's call for volunteers and did their rudimentary training around 'Bostock's Jungle', 'Bristol Castle' and Drake's ship 'Revenge', were lost to their loved ones for ever.

WHITE CITY LIVES ON

One of the original volunteers who did return home was Gilbert Dicks. He enlisted at the Colston Hall on 12th September 1914 aged just 17. He was shot in the leg on 3rd September 1916 at Guillemont, during the Battle of the Somme. He and his platoon went 'over the top' at 12 noon and most were killed or injured within half-an-hour. In a memoir discovered at Bristol Record Office, Dicks described how, with the assistance of a German prisoner, he made his way back to Maricourt where ambulances were waiting to take the injured to hospital.

Once he'd recovered, he was drafted into the 1st

Pte Gilbert Dicks, second from the right on Guard Duty at White City Barracks in 1915.

Gloucesters in December 1916 and joined the Signal Section. He served with the Battalion for the rest of the war and following the Armistice entered Germany in January 1919. Later in the month he was demobilised and returned home to Bristol to find work.

For a while the White City barracks was used as a dispersal depot for troops, but for some, the frustration of being confined got too much. On 7th January 1919 around 120 Royal Engineers who were attached to the 12th Battalion, Bedfordshire Regiment marched out of the barracks and on to the Council House. They wanted to get back to their Croydon depot and return to civilian life. The Lord Mayor received a deputation in his offices and promised to put their case to the authorities.

A week later, the Engineers had left the site and the great White City sell-off began. Auctions under the direction of the Surplus Government Property Disposal Board got underway immediately. Lorries and cars, motor bikes with side cars, sporting and gym equipment, concrete block buildings, two mini hospital units, a fumigation room and a disinfector all came under the hammer at Messrs Miller & Brown's salesroom in Bristol. Even the three billiard tables provided for the troops in the Writing and Recreation room were sold off for £156.

Some of the buildings, like the strengthened Bristol Castle and the Dominions building were used for warehouse storage during the 1920s, but by 1930, even these structures had been removed.

During the Second World War, Gilbert Dicks did

his bit again and was a voluntary instructor in Air Raid Precautions and First Aid for Air Raid Casualties. The White City site again played host to the military with the War Office utilising part of the site for a military camp. Several huts were built on the site and on a nearby one at Bower Ashton where they accommodated HM and Allied units.

For a time American soldiers like James T Barr of the 109th Finance Disbursing Section were based at the White City camp and he recalled cycle rides to and from the camp and returning in the blackout from evenings at the movies or a visit to the American Red Cross… *"We always hoped the Swing Bridge would be where it was supposed to be and not open causing a delay getting back to the wonders of the White City camp…"*

After the D-Day landings many local camps and those in Ashton became home to German POWs.

Kathleen Woodward who lived in Bower Road, Ashton recalled that there were a number of POW camps in the area. The Germans were often seen in the neighbourhood walking around in their distinctive POW uniforms. Some of the neighbours befriended them which she remembered caused some bad feeling, as they were encouraged to try and sell small wooden toys they had made in the camp. She remembered when two of the POWs leaned on her front gate looking at her little sister playing and her mother rushed out and took her into the house. Towards the end of the war the German speakers in her class at school were taken to a hall in Bedminster to entertain German prisoners by singing German carols, and taking around refreshments.

One of the German POWs in Ashton, Harald Gorling, was befriended by Gilbert Dicks and his wife. Perhaps

Bristol school girls at the derelict White City camp just after the Second World War.

Dicks remembered the assistance he received 30 years earlier when helped from the Somme Battlefield by a German prisoner. Gilbert Dicks and his wife entertained Harald Gorling on several occasions and welcomed him into their home on Christmas Day 1946. Gorling left Bristol in around March 1947 and following a short spell in a transit camp in Colchester, returned home to a devastated Hannover on 26th April 1947.

The Dicks family sent Gorling on his way with some presents for his wife. Writing to the Dicks family in 1947, Gorling said… *"Too bad you could not be with us when we were unpacking. You should have seen the face of my wife when I brought into daylight your presents. She cried of joy and could hardly grasp that there are still people helping so altruistically strangers who are in want. The dress, the shoes and all the other clothing fit like made for*

White City squatters take up residence on 14th August 1946.

her. As my wife, since she was totally bombed out in March 1945, possessed nothing but the things she was wearing, you can imagine her surprise and joy. My wife thanks you with all her heart for the wonderful presents and sends you her kindest regards…"

Bristol had much in common with Hannover. The bombing of both cities left thousands of people without homes and Bristol residents along with families across the country took the law into their own hands. During the summer of 1946, thousands of British families began to "requisition" empty military camps. Within two weeks almost all of the country's vacant military sites had been partially or completely occupied. In all but a few cases, the squatters were permitted to stay. Within three months, management of the camps was handed over to local authorities, who provided services and collected rents.

There were a large number of former British and US military sites in and around Bristol and with 26,000 names on the council waiting list, the housing situation for ordinary Bristolians was pretty dire. Early in 1946, Councillor Alfred Duggan who represented Bedminster, waged an energetic campaign in the Council chamber and in the local press for the White City camp to be used for housing. He argued that the buildings would make excellent temporary homes.

Picking up the mood, Alderman Henry Hennessy, a member of the Housing Committee, announced on Monday 12th August 1946 that he would be at the White City camp at 7.30pm the following evening to "meet any families contemplating moving into the huts and to help them select the best."

Hennessy's announcement prompted some to jump the gun. On the Monday evening, a small crowd gathered at the camp gate. "Wait until tomorrow," said one man, "and there will be many more down here. Then some of us who are desperate won't stand a chance."

They crossed the barrier to be met by the camp warden who said that although he sympathised with them it was his job to protect government property. He then called the police. An inspector, a sergeant and three constables arrived and the inspector warned the crowd that they were trespassing and advised them not to do any damage.

People surged into the camp, racing to stake their claims to the best huts. Little or no damage was done; some huts were entered through windows, others had keys in the doors. Around 30 people slept on the floors of the huts they had claimed and moved their furniture and belongings in the following day. They elected a

Squatters with bedding and pet cat on the White City site and about to claim a derelict hut for themselves, 14th August 1946.

management committee and agreed to pay 6s per week per household into a rent fund.

On Tuesday 13th August 1946, Alderman Hennessy, addressed the White City squatters. "We have captured our objectives," and described the squatters' action as "invasion – but with no hostility" and "requisitioning by the people".

A similar 'requisitioning' had taken place at the end of 1919. Thomas Inskip, MP for Bristol Central, asked Winston Churchill, Secretary of State for War, whether he could hasten the vacation of some of the land occupied by the military authorities at the White City site. The owners of the land were willing to allow a new allotments association, composed largely of ex-servicemen, to let the land for cultivation.

Churchill knocked some heads together and the White City Allotments were born – the name is the only remaining link with the past.

PICTURE CREDITS

KEY   BRO = Bristol Record Office   BLS = Bristol Library Service   SoGM = Soldiers of Gloucestershire Museum

P4	BRO 43207/22/3/8
P6	Author's own collection

PART 1

P10	BRO 40156/14 Vol III No 4
P12	BRO PicBox/6/Misc/40
P13	BRO 43207/9/4/37
P15	BRO-PBA-Corp-E3-101
P21	BRO 40156/15 Vol III No 5
P25	BRO – 43207/22/3/1
P26/27	BRO 37165/7/3
P28	BRO 43207/9/30/137
P29	BRO 43207/22/3/4
P30	BRO 43207/22/3/2
P31	BRO 43207/22/3/3
P33 (left)	BRO 40156/14 Vol III No4
P33 (right)	BLS – Loxton N982
P34	BRO 43207/22/3/29
P35	BRO 43207/22/3/24
P37	BRO 43207/22/3/16
P38	BRO 43207/9/4/42
P40 (left)	BRO 13758/2
P40 (right)	BLS B14511
P41	BRO 43207/22/3/25
P42	BRO 43207/9/4/39/2
P43	BRO 43207/22/3/23
P45 (top)	BRO 43207/23/3/12
P45 (bottom)	BRO 43207/9/4/40
P47	BRO 43207/9/4/53
P48	BRO 43207/9/4/46
P49	BRO 43207/22/3/19
P53	BRO Pamphlet 669
P54 (top)	BRO 43207/9/4/57
P54 (bottom)	BRO 43207/22/11/3
P55	BRO 43207/9/4/60
P56	BRO 43207/9/4/62
P57 (top)	BRO 43207/9/4/61
P57 (bottom)	BRO 43207/22/11/4

PART 2

P61	Author's own collection
P62	BRO 43207/7/1/3
P63	BRO 9314
P64	BRO 40715/Pers/SCB/8/6/9
P65	Andy Stevens, Pastimes
P67	BLS and BRO 12631/16
P68	SoGM
P69 (top)	BRO 40353/8(m)
P69 (bottom)	BRO 43207/8/51
P70 (left)	BRO 43207/8/50
P70 (right)	BRO 43207/8/27
P71	BRO 43207/9/68
P72	BRO 43207/8/30
P72	badge, courtesy of Peter John
P73	Andy Stevens, Pastimes
P74	BRO 43207/8/81
P75	BLS B248 Vol I 132
P76	BRO 43207/8/63
P77	Andy Stevens, Pastimes
P78	BRO 43207/8/24
P79	BRO 43207/8/37
P80	And Stevens, Pastimes
P81	BRO 44859/3-p41
P82	Andy Stevens, Pastimes
P83	Andy Stevens, Pastimes
P84	Andy Stevens, Pastimes
P85	BRO 43207/8/38
P86	SoGM
P87	Andy Stevens, Pastimes
P89	Andy Stevens, Pastimes
P90	Pamela Steed
P91	Pamela Steed
P92	BRO 42601
P93	Bristol Post
P94	Bristol Post
P95	Bristol Post